WRITING IN
SUBJECT-MATTER FIELDS:

A Bibliographic Guide, with

Annotations and Writing Assignments

compiled by

EVA M. BURKETT

The Scarecrow Press, Inc.
Metuchen, N.J.   1977

Library of Congress Cataloging in Publication Data

Burkett, Eva Mae.
    Writing in subject-matter fields.

    Includes index.
    1.   English language--Rhetoric--Study and teaching--
Bibliography.   I.   Title.
Z2015.R5B87   [PE1404]   016.808'042   76-30397
ISBN 0-8108-1012-3

CONTENTS

INTRODUCTION

WRITING IN RELATION TO
READING AND THINKING

Many colleges and universities throughout the country have dropped Freshman Composition as a requirement, but departments other than English still demand, or suggest, or hope, that their students be able to express themselves in writing. This demand is being met in various ways, and sometimes not at all. Some universities have writing laboratories conducted by the English departments to help students with their writing problems. Other institutions have tutorial services and courses in the fundamentals of English. But tutorial teaching is expensive, and if the teaching is done by student assistants, the instruction is apt to be poor. There is also a tendency in such instruction to concentrate on mechanics and on solving the problems of a particular writing assignment rather than on the principles of writing.

A course in writing for college students should not be a "service" course, a course in writing skills, or a course in drills on usage or on errors to be avoided. It should be a course that demands of the student the use of his best powers of thinking and of his knowledge and experience in all fields of study. The course should show him that he must control his material, through organization, through syntactical structure, and through word choice, if he expects to control the responses of his reader. He must learn that effective writing is not something he can toss off in a moment of inspiration but that it requires careful planning and thinking and revising. It is the result of a search for order and for making the best choices. Writing on this level is a liberal study, a way of working through shoddy or surface thinking, a way by which one discovers ideas and transmits what he discovers. Writing helps to clarify thinking, and straight thinking demands clear verbal expression. It may even help to create ideas, for one does not always know what he thinks until he attempts to put his ideas into written form.

John C. Mellon makes an even stronger plea for writing: "In pondering the value of writing, whether to the college bound or the early school leaver, regardless of fancies as to its 'practical' value or the current extent of its use for hire, we should always be mindful of the truth long recognized by scholars of language and thought, that writing is the greatest tool of thinking ever invented by man." ("Round Two of the National Writing Assessment-Interpreting the Apparent Decline of Writing Ability: A Review," Research in the Teaching of English, X, No. 1 (Spring, 1976), 73.)

A feeling of power and freedom comes to the student when he is able to express his ideas effectively. No longer is he dependent on the clichés and ready-made phrases that are the marks of our "blurb-oriented" society. He experiences pleasure in using his own mind and in making words and sentences and paragraphs obey his will. He learns to adapt language to his purpose and to his audience and to make his writing clear, lively, and convincing. His pleasure in writing leads him to examine and to evaluate the methods and techniques in what he reads and to see the relation between the way an idea is expressed and its effect. He notices that a difference in linguistic form assures a difference in meaning. Thus he comes to see that language is not a dull, lifeless subject but may be a part of an exciting creative process. He learns that reading is not only a pleasure in itself but is also an aid to writing. He will now read for overtones and arrangement of words as well as for ideas and for information.

In order to read with understanding and appreciation of what one reads, the individual should have the following knowledge and abilities:

1. A sufficient knowledge of grammatical relationships to distinguish sentence elements and to recognize sentence items that are in parallel positions.

2. A sufficient acquaintance with historical events and characters, Biblical stories and characters, literature, mythology, etc., to relate references in these areas to the purpose and meaning of the writing being studied, or a knowledge of how to obtain such background information and the curiosity and energy to obtain it.

3. The recognition of language change and the ability to derive a particular meaning of a word from the context or

from dictionaries that show the history of the meaning of words.

4. The ability to observe and to trace thematic elements and motifs.

5. The ability to recognize levels of meaning as shown in such devices as symbols, tone, language forms, rhythm.

6. The ability to distinguish between what a writer says and what he may mean in ironical and satirical writing.

7. The ability to recognize and to evaluate devices of persuasion and to detect fallacies, if any, in the writer's thinking and presentation.

8. The ability to distinguish early in the writing the author's purpose and design and to distinguish the ideas of the author from those he may assign to his characters. The reader should also be able to recognize instances of the author's incomplete success in achieving his design.

9. The ability to understand the use of metaphorical language.

10. The ability to apply particular methods of reading to particular kinds of writing. One does not read a newspaper with the same concentration as he may apply to a philosophical treatise.

11. The energy for multiple readings: for total effect, for attention to particular aspects, for sound and rhythm, for attention to structure and language, to key words and sentences.

The personal traits of a good reader may be summarized as follows:

1. He assumes responsibility for contributing his own knowledge and abilities to understanding the writing. He does not expect the writer to make every idea simple and clear to him since complex ideas may demand complex presentation.

2. He has formed the habit of reading widely and with purpose. He reads outside his major interest since he realizes that all knowledge is a part of a large body of interrelated knowledge.

3. He has the persistence that makes him work at understanding what is not readily discernible to him. He derives pleasure from working at interpretation.

Since writing is not confined to English courses and since the broad principles of writing are the same in all fields--selecting and limiting the subject, indicating the purpose of writing, developing the subject to accomplish the purpose, and deciding on a way of writing that is in keeping with the subject and purpose--the material in this bibliography has been chosen to give the student not only general ideas about writing, but also the opinions of successful writers in various subject-matter fields. A particular feature of the bibliography is Chapter 6, which is concerned with the relationships of writing in several subject-matter fields, for ideas and forms are not isolated nor confined but include the whole spectrum of intellectual activity.

The bibliography will be useful for class instruction, for seminar groups, for individuals working on projects in particular fields, or for anyone interested in learning more about what accomplished writers say about writing. It will also serve as a convenient reference in writing laboratories. The writing assignments are not designed as daily busy work, but as problems that involve reading and thinking that should lead to carefully-planned and carefully-written papers that require some time in preparation. Since a writer must have something to write about, much of the material in several of the articles and in many of the assignments is concerned with subject matter for writing. Only in the sense that all writing is creative can the writing assignments be labeled as creative writing. The emphasis is on expository writing. It is hoped that the book will be used by experienced teachers who know something of the nature of language and its use in effective written expression instead of by untrained student assistants who may lack not only knowledge of the principles of writing but also experience in directing students in thinking and in expression. The book is not intended for use with remedial groups unless the instructor knows that writing comes from interest in ideas and their expression, and not from drill on usage and comma faults.

E. M. B.

CHAPTER 1

ABOUT WRITING

Attitudes toward Writing
Writers on Writing
Interviews with Writers

"It is our belief that no writer can improve his work until he discards the dulcet notion that the reader is feeble-minded, for writing is an act of faith, not a trick of grammar. Ascent is at the heart of the matter. A country whose writers are following a calculating machine downstairs is not ascending--if you will pardon the expression--and a writer who questions the capacity of the person at the other end of the line is not a writer at all, merely a schemer. The movies long ago decided that a wider communication could be achieved by a deliberate descent to a lower level, and they walked proudly down until they reached the cellar. Now they are groping for the light switch, hoping to find a way out."

--E. B. White, "Calculating Machine," in The Second Tree from the Corner. New York: Harper and Brothers, 1951, pp. 166-167.

"... to write well, even to write clearly, is a woundy business, long to learn, hard to learn, and no gift of the angels. Style should not obtrude between a writer and his reader; it must be the servant, not master. To use words so true and simple that they oppose no obstacle to the flow of thought and feeling from mind to mind, and yet by juxtaposition of word-sounds set up in the recipient continuing emotion or gratification--that is the essence of style."

--John Galsworthy, "Foreword," to W. H. Hudson, Green Mansions. New York: Random House, 1944, p. ix.

"When you write, you make a point, not by subtracting as though you sharpened a pencil, but by adding. When you put one word after another, your statement should be more precise the more you add. If the result is otherwise, you have added the wrong thing, or you have added more than was needed."

--John Erskine, "A Note on the Writer's Craft," in Twentieth Century English. Edited by William S. Knickerbocker. Freeport, N.Y.: Books for Libraries Press, p. 254. Copyright by Philosophical Library, Inc., 1946.

"But the writer is the eyes and ears of his reader, and those eyes and ears must be alert today as never before, in order to show the reader the facts on which he will ultimately base his judgments. In a world where practically the only uncomplex thing is the cliché about that world's growing complexity, the writer's task is to make what sense he can out of the tangled mass of detail that is the only valid source of any generalization. "

--James F. Fixx, "Is Greatness Everything?" Saturday Review, November 17, 1962, p. 24.

"Any discipline can help your writing: logic, mathematics, theology, and of course and particularly drawing. Anything that helps you to see, anything that makes you look. The writer should never be ashamed of staring. There is nothing that doesn't require his attention. "

--Flannery O'Connor, "The Nature and Aim of Fiction, " in The Writer's Craft. Edited by John Hersey. New York: Alfred A. Knopf, 1974, p. 55.

"To the extent that we think in words, language is an instrument of perception as well as of expression. A thought we can't express is one that we don't quite understand, not having worked it out. Working it out involves constructing it as a sentence or a series of sentences. If we lack the appropriate words, and have little skill in the syntactic arrangement of such words as we have, not only can we not express nuances of thought and feeling, we can't even experience them. "

--J. Mitchell Morse, "Why Write Like a College Graduate?" College English, XXXII (October, 1970), 6.

ATTITUDES TOWARD WRITING

Although it is probably true that English teachers on both high school and college levels continue to spend the major part of their composition teaching in emphasizing grammatical forms and usage, not a single author of the twenty-seven articles included in this section mentions correctness as the goal of writing. The writers emphasize the importance of having something to say, of keeping the audience in mind, of using language with clarity and precision, of writing as an intellectual activity, and of learning to write by constant writing and revising. Several of the writers stress the relation between one's use of language and personal efficiency in the conduct of one's own affairs as well as in the management of national and international interests; others mention the importance of reading not only for information but for understanding how technique helps to discover and to present ideas.

1. Barloon, Marvin J. "How to Teach Students to Write Clearly in Courses Other Than English," American Association of University Professors Bulletin, XXXIX (Autumn, 1953), 286-292.

An account of the method developed by the author for teaching his students in Industrial Economics to write acceptable papers. Barloon's method is based on four principles: teach the student the elements of a performance before teaching the whole performance; show the student what you are trying to teach him to do before expecting him to do it; show the student what he has done wrong and be sure that he understands the criticism before asking him to correct it; judge a student's ability to write by the fact that he can carry out an assignment without interference or guidance from his instructor.

2. Booth, Wayne G. "The Rhetorical Stance," College Composition and Communication, XIV (October, 1963), 138-145.

Booth says that English teachers at all levels have a

special responsibility to get certain basic principles into all writing assignments. The common ingredient that Booth finds in the writing he admires, except in novels, plays, and poems, is what he calls the "rhetorical stance," the maintaining of a proper balance among the arguments about the subject, the interests and peculiarities of the audience, and the implied character of the speaker.

3. Burling, Robbins. "An Anthropologist among the English Teachers," College Composition and Communication, XXV (October, 1974), 234-242.

Burling, an anthropologist from the University of Michigan, describes his own Freshman English course as "dismal." He thinks that most composition courses suffer from two weaknesses: concentration on trivia, such as spelling and commas, and "mushy libertarianism," where the teacher is afraid of stifling the student's "own voice." Burling tells how he learned to write a senior thesis, graduate term papers, and a dissertation, but it was another anthropologist, not an English teacher, who gave him his first effective lesson in English composition. He thinks that the teaching of English composition should not be the task of English teachers only, but that every teacher of every subject should share this burden. He suggests as the two prerequisites for any decent writing course a focus on rewriting and a realistic choice of topics for writing (he deplores the personal experience paper). He lists twelve categories of exercises that he thinks would be helpful to students, but his main advice is for students to spend much time in rewriting.

4. Channing, Edward T. Lectures Read to the Seniors in Harvard College. Edited by Dorothy I. Anderson and Waldo W. Braden. Foreword by David Potter. Carbondale and Edwardsville: Southern Illinois University Press, 1968, 303 pp. Offset from the first edition of Lectures on Rhetoric, published in 1856.

Channing was Boylston Professor of Rhetoric and Oratory at Harvard, 1819-1851. Although at this time rhetoric meant primarily speaking and oratory, Channing also taught the theory and practice of writing. Three of the lectures included in the volume are of interest to students of writing. In "A Writer's Preparation," Channing says that an improvement does take place in the writing of college students, but the improvement is gradual and is due to a "revolution" that takes place in the minds of the students to which the exercises of the rhetoric class contribute their influence. "No modest teacher would claim to have made his pupil a good

writer; and no prudent one ... would undertake to say how it
was effected. " In "Writer's Habits," Channing says that writing as an exercise in college does more than make the writer
skillful in composition, for it gives students "habits of self-
denial, industry and close study, a general and ready command of our faculties, a clear, direct way of thinking on all
subjects and occasions, a promptness and decision in our
opinions, and a natural and precise method of expressing
them. " In "Clearness of Expression and Thought," Channing
emphasizes precision in writing which he thinks can be accomplished by the habit of putting thoughts on paper.

5. Ciardi, John. "What Every Writer Must Learn,"
in Dialogue with an Audience. Philadelphia: J. B. Lippincott Company, 1963, pp. 252-261.
According to Ciardi, creativity cannot be taught but
the elements of creation can be learned. He discusses six
elements that a good writer must have: a knowledge of facts;
a sense of aesthetic detachment that enables a writer "to ride
his passion" while observing it critically; technical and emotional fluency; a knowledge of what has been accomplished in
the past in the art form in which he is writing and the ability
to read as a professional, that is, with an understanding of
the ideas as well as with an awareness of the technical management; an understanding of his own times, a sense of his
age, its moods, its ideas, its human position, and its potential for action; the recognition that art is a made representation of life and not life itself.

6. Craft So Hard to Learn. Conversations with Poets
and Novelists about the Teaching of Writing. Conducted by
John Graham and George Garrett. New York: William Mor-
row and Company, 1972, 95 pp. (Paper)
A collection of interviews with eleven writers who
served as members of the writing staff of the Hollins Conference in Creative Writing and Cinema, June 15-27, 1970.
Each of the conversations comes from a fifteen-minute tape
recording. Graham is the interviewer and Garrett the editor.
All of the writers are teachers of writing.

7. Erskine, John. "A Note on the Writer's Craft,"
in Twentieth Century English. Edited by William S. Knickerbocker. Freeport, N.Y.: Books for Libraries Press, 1970,
pp. 251-259. Philosophical Library, 1946.
Erskine says that when you write, you make a point
by adding, not by subtracting, and that your statement becomes more precise the more you add if you add the right

thing or do not add more than is needed. Sentences are
added on the same principle as are words and the last sentence of the paragraph completes the meaning. The place
for ending is determined by the writer. Where a work begins depends on the reader. Thus composition can be taught
only when the student is aware of his audience.

8. Estrin, Herman A. "Motivation in Composition
Writing," Improving College and University Teaching, XXI
(Spring, 1973), 132-134.

Estrin, Associate Chairman of the Department of Humanities, Newark College of Engineering, says that students
write best on topics in which they are interested. He suggests that in assigning topics for composition, teachers
should know the abilities, interests, and goals of their students and should make writing assignments on topics that are
relevant, meaningful, and interesting to students. After
being graded and commented on by the teacher and revised
by the students, the compositions should be suitable for publication.

9. Gibson, Walker. "Composition as the Center for
an Intellectual Life," in The Hues of English. NCTE 1969
Distinguished Lectures. Champaign, Illinois: National
Council of Teachers of English, 1969, pp. 73-90.

Walker Gibson says that the central concern of the
teacher of composition is to increase the range of his students' options as writers, to enable the writer to inspire
trust in what he is writing about; in short, to establish belief in his character as it is expressed in prose.

10. Johnson, Wendell. "You Can't Write Writing,"
in The Use and Abuse of Language. Edited by S. I. Hayakawa. Greenwich, Conn.: Fawcett Publications, 1952, pp.
101-111.

Johnson's experience with graduate students convinced
him that English teachers have placed emphasis upon writing
rather than upon writing about something for someone. He
offers a few principles of effective writing: clearness depends upon agreement between the writer and his readers as
to what the words of the writer represent; the organization
of what one writes should correspond to the organization of
what he is writing about; attention should be paid to logical
transitions; clarity is a prerequisite to validity. Johnson
says that the ability to use language clearly and with validity
is basic not only to personal efficiency and to individual
sanity, but is also fundamental to the proper management of
national and international problems.

11. Lucas, F. L. "Methods of Writing," in Style. New York: Macmillan, 1955. Collier Books, 1962, pp. 215-275.

Lucas's suggestions as to methods of writing fall into three stages: meditation and documentation, incubation; periods of alternate thought, quick writing, and partial revision; revision, with further documentation, correction, curtailment, and amplification. He advises the writer to pursue clarity and brevity, and to be courteous to readers; never to write a line without considering whether it is really true and without exaggeration; to shun dead images and cherish living ones; to revise "unremittingly."

12. McCrimmon, James M. "Writing as a Way of Knowing," in The Promise of English. NCTE 1970 Distinguished Lectures. Champaign, Ill.: National Council of Teachers of English, 1970, pp. 117-130.

McCrimmon views writing not in the customary way of the writer having something to say to the reader, but as a means that the writer has of finding out what he wants to say. Writing as a way of knowing emphasizes the quality of what is presented, while writing as a way of telling emphasizes the quality of the presentation. McCrimmon points out that too much teaching of writing is concerned with usage, with "correctness." He mentions the importance of class discussion about how a writing assignment can be carried out before actual writing begins.

13. Morse, J. Mitchell. "Why Write Like a College Graduate?" College English, XXXII (October, 1970), 1-8.

Since we think in words, the quality of our thinking inheres in our language. It is thus essential, says Morse, that students be aroused to an emotional concern for clarity and precision in their use of language as a means of defending and rescuing our civilization from destruction by promoting the elements of thought.

14. Namier, Lewis Berstein. "English Prose," in Conflicts: Studies in Contemporary History. London, 1942. Books for Libraries Press, 1969, pp. 217-223.

Because of its mixed origin, the English language is a perfect instrument for expressing ideas clearly or for being evasive as the need arises. Namier advises writers to suit style to purpose, to avoid verbiage, to handle pronouns with care, to cut out meanderings, repetition, signposts, and announcements, and to leave a margin for the thought of the reader.

15. Ong, Walter J. S. J. "The Writer's Audience Is Always a Fiction," PMLA, XC (January, 1975), 9-21.

Ong says that he means two things when he says that the audience is always a fiction: the writer must construct in his imagination an audience cast in some sort of role, and the reader must also fictionalize himself, that is, he must play the role in which the author casts him. In these respects, he does not exclude history, scientific writing, familiar letters, diaries, and confessional literature.

16. Scully, Malcolm G. "Crisis in English Writing," Chronicle of Higher Education, IX, No. 1 (September 23, 1974), 1, 6.

Scully says that many students who are entering colleges today are "functionally illiterate" and that many college English departments and college English teachers are doing little to remedy the situation. He cites Robert F. Hogan, executive secretary of the National Council of Teachers of English, who says that it is possible for a student to go all the way through high school, through college, and into the teaching profession without having had a course in composition after the ninth grade. Some English departments are being forced by students who want colleges to provide them with vocational skills to examine their heretofore total commitment to literature and to include composition as part of their program.

17. Smith, Adam. Lectures on Rhetoric and Belles Lettres. Delivered in the University of Glasgow. Reported by a Student in 1762-63. Edited with an Introduction and Notes by John M. Lothian. Foreword by David Potter. Carbondale and Edwardsville: Southern Illinois University Press, 1971. 205 pp.

A collection of 29 lectures by Adam Smith to students at the University of Glasgow from notes kept by a student. The lectures, given November 19, 1762 to February 18, 1763, are concerned with the principles of good composition, narrative writing and description in historical writing, discussions of the work of certain historians, expository writing, and judicial oratory.

18. Smith, Charlotte Watkins. "The Art of Writing," in Carl Becker: On History and the Climate of Opinion. Ithaca, N.Y.: Cornell University Press, 1956, pp. 131-166.

Smith discusses Becker's ideas of writing as they are given in his manuscript on "The Art of Writing," and explains Becker's peculiar ability as a writer under the following heads:

he had the urge to write; he had the habit of reading, not
only for information but for the meaning, the overtones, and
the sounds of words; he avoided ugly compound words; and
he studied such craftsmen as Aristotle, Virginia Woolf,
Marcel Proust, and especially Henry James, Remy de Gour-
mont, and Pascal. Becker's most important advice to
writers is to learn to write through writing, through keeping
journals, and through filing notes of ideas and reflections.
He believed that the idea should determine the form and the
style should suit the writer.

19. Struck, H. R. "Wanted: More Writing Courses
for Graduate Students," College Composition and Communication, XXVII (May, 1976), 192-197.
Struck advocates a course in writing for graduate students, for, he says, his experience shows that eight or nine
out of ten Ph.D. students will improve their writing signifi-
cantly, but only three or four out of ten undergraduates will
improve. The chief reason for improvement is motivation.
The key feature of the course that Struck teaches at Michigan
State University is the use of frequency counts for analyzing
a student's style and for recommending changes if they are
needed.

20. Tibbetts, A. M. "To Encourage Reason on the
Campus: A Proposal for a New College Course in Thinking
and Writing," American Association of University Professors
Bulletin, LIV (Winter, 1968), 466-472.
Tibbetts makes a plea for a new college course for
all freshmen to replace the old freshman composition course,
to be called Investigating, Thinking, and Arguing, that would
teach students to investigate and look into subjects; to evaluate
evidence and authority; to learn the major logical and verbal
fallacies and how to avoid them; and to present in written
form a rigorous, logical, sequential, and factual argument,
with specific reasons for supporting, attacking, or critically
analyzing a particular thesis.

21. Wendell, Barrett. English Composition. New
York: Charles Scribner's Sons, 1908. 316 pp.
A collection of eight lectures, given at the Lowell
Institute, that constitute the course in English Composition
that Wendell taught freshman students at Harvard for more
than ten years before he organized his ideas about writing
into his now famous textbook. The lectures are concerned
with the elements and qualities of style; with words, sentences, paragraphs, and whole compositions; as well as with

clearness, force, and elegance. Wendell opposes the teaching of composition as an "empty abstraction," but thinks that it should be taught in relation to other fields of study.

22. Wendell, Barrett. "The Study of Expression," in The Mystery of Education and Other Academic Performances. New York: Charles Scribner's Sons, 1909. Freeport, N.Y.: Books for Libraries Press, 1971, pp. 137-194.
A commencement address given at the College of Charleston, South Carolina, June 15, 1909, in which Wendell discusses the course in composition that he taught at Harvard. He says that the principles of composition studied by themselves become sterile, for composition implies a fusion of thought and emotion gained from learning and experience. He thinks that a writer expresses himself best when he says what he means, when he holds the attention of his audience, and when he engages the sympathy of those who attend.

23. Wright, Palmer. "Advanced Composition Courses and the Current University Crisis," Proceedings of Conference of College Teachers of English in Texas, XXVIII (September, 1973), 48-53.
Wright advocates moving the second-semester composition course from the freshman to the junior level. This, he says, will allow the student to apply to his advanced knowledge of some subject the rhetorical principles learned in the first-semester course, and the writing course can be designed to meet the need of the student in his chosen field. To meet this need, he proposes four advanced courses: "Composition and Rhetoric in the Study of Literature and the Arts," "The Logic and Rhetoric of Expository Writing," "Writing in American Studies," and "Writing Problems in the Social Studies." These courses would be in addition to the two usual advanced courses--creative and technical writing.

24. "The Writing Gap," Yale Alumni Magazine, January, 1976, pp. 16-26.
This is a series of four articles concerned with the inability of students to express themselves clearly in writing: "Sentimentality," by A. Bartlett Giamatti, Professor of English and Comparative Literature at Yale; "Bonehead English," by Paula Johnson, Associate Professor of English and Director of Undergraduate Studies in the English Department; "Jargon" by William Kessen, Professor of Psychology and Research Associate in Pediatrics; and "Blame," by H. Mark Johnson, teacher of English and History at the Hammonasset School.

In "Sentimentality," Giamatti says that present-day college students cannot write because, as grammar and high school students of the 1960's and early 1970's, they have lost touch with the language through the "anti-structures" movements of the time. The Free Speech Movement tended "to free us from the shackles of syntax, the racism of grammar, the elitism of style." This distrust of the restrictions of language is the main reason why young people today cannot write. Giamatti says that since language is the means by which the race lives, a group of people who cannot clearly and precisely speak and write will never be a genuine society.

In "Bonehead English," Paula Johnson discusses the courses offered to freshman students over the last several years by the Yale English Department and the new version of English 10 that will be offered next fall. This course is a review of English grammar and the usual emphasis on the techniques of composition and the mechanics of writing.

William Kessen says in "Jargon" that the social sciences have grown a special language, a jargon or dialect used to identify other members of the group, thereby preventing the layman from understanding what is meant. He thinks, however, "there is room for tough, perceptive prose even in psychology."

In "Blame," H. Mark Johnson agrees that students cannot write, but he questions the assumption that the educational system is primarily to blame for poor student writers. One cause, he says, is the inability or reluctance of teachers to let their students do much writing because of their load of 150 to 180 students each term. Some teachers also equate teaching writing with "learning parts of speech, diagramming sentences, memorizing vocabulary lists, filling out book report forms and practicing sample questions for the SAT's." Other causes of poor writing, he says, are the early environment of the child, the complexity and illogic of the English language, and the fact that some students have a linguistic "tin ear." There is also disagreement over what inability to write really means. Johnson says that since it is impossible for any one academic department to prepare students to write acceptable, imaginative expository prose in all of the disciplines, the teaching of writing should be the domain of the whole faculty and we should think of learning to write as a life-long process. He says that we should also return to the idea that form and content are inseparable. "An intelligent idea can be lost because of inept form; excessive concentration on form can stifle creative content."

WRITING ASSIGNMENTS

1. Read the interviews with teachers of writing in Craft So Hard to Learn and write a paper in which you present the ideas about writing expressed by these author-teachers. Organize your material so that you discuss in the same section the ideas on particular topics by all of the writers.

2. Walker Gibson says that a concern for politics can be a concern for language, that one must understand one's politics through language. Choose a speech of some well-known political figure and write a paper in which you analyze his character as it is shown in the language he uses in the speech.

3. After reading "You Can't Write Writing," write a paper in which you apply Johnson's idea that the use of language with clearness and with validity is basic to personal efficiency and to the adequate management of our national and international affairs. Use individual examples where possible. To what extent was the misuse of language responsible for the Watergate debacle? You may want to read the articles in Language and Politics (see Chapter 6) before you begin.

4. In his discussion of the writer's audience, Walter Ong makes several references to Hemingway as an example of how a writer fictionalizes the reader. Read a section from one of Hemingway's novels or stories and write a paper in which you describe the fictionalized reader. Or, you may choose another kind of writing--history, scientific writing, letters, diaries, etc.--and write a paper describing the fictionalized reader. In either paper, point out the basis for your comments from the writing.

5. After reading "Crisis in English Writing," write a paper in which you present your views on the current crisis and describe the kind of writing program that you think will best fit your future needs.

6. Write a paper in which you present your opinions on the course that Tibbetts would like to see replace the regular freshman composition course. You may want to comment on your own freshman composition course as a basis of comparison.

7. After reading Barrett Wendell's English

Composition and "A Study of Expression," write a paper in
which you compare Wendell's ideas of composition with the
ideas of the more modern writers included in this list. You
may want to read also Barrett Wendell and His Letters,
edited by M. A. DeWolfe Howe, 1924; and Essays in Memory
of Barrett Wendell, 1926. Or, you may compare the attitudes toward writing expressed by outstanding teachers of
writing around the end of the nineteenth century with those
of teachers of the present time. For this purpose, in addition to Wendell, you may use such teachers as John Franklin
Genung, Professor of Rhetoric, Amherst, who wrote The
Working Principles of Rhetoric, Examined in Their Literary
Relations and Illustrated with Examples, 1900; John Duncan
Quackenbos, Columbia University, author of Practical Rhe-
toric, 1896; and Arnold Tompkins, Professor of Pedagogy,
University of Illinois, author of The Science of Discourse.
A Rhetoric for High Schools and Colleges, 1889.

"Writing is a lonely occupation at best. Of course there are stimulating and even happy associations with friends and colleagues, but during the actual work of creation the writer cuts himself off from all others and confronts his subject alone. He moves into a realm where he has never been before--perhaps where no one has ever been. It is a lonely place, and even a little frightening."

--Rachel Carson, Acceptance Speech for Achievement Award of American Association of University Women. Quoted in The House of Life. Rachel Carson at Work, by Paul Brooks. Boston: Houghton Mifflin Company, 1972, p. 1.

"Is all writing in place of doing? Necessarily, I suppose, but it is something else, too. Among other things it's a way of remembering."

--John Ciardi, "Manner of Speaking," Saturday Review, October 16, 1971, p. 24.

"It is easier to write about writing than it is to write the sort of writing that ought to be written about."

--John Hersey, "The Novel of Contemporary History," Atlantic Monthly, LCXXXIV (1949), 84.

WRITERS ON WRITING

The writers in this section are primarily concerned with the art of writing and with the relation of this art to the design and technique of the completed work. Many of them stress the importance of practice in writing and of constant revision. Others mention the value of keeping a notebook for ideas, while others emphasize wide reading, continued study, and attention to language. Several mention the value of early experience and of memory as material for writing. Purpose in writing varies with the writer. One writer suggests that some write for the freedom they find in the creation of a bearable world. Another says that he writes from political impulse, the desire to change society. Practically all of the writers mention that writing is hard work and requires both mental and physical discipline.

1. Barry, Elaine. Robert Frost on Writing. New Brunswick, N.J.: Rutgers University Press, 1973. 188 pp.
A collection of letters, reviews, prefaces, lectures, and interviews by Robert Frost on the craft of writing, some of which go back to 1913. Many of Frost's comments on writing poetry also apply to the writing of good prose.

2. Borges on Writing. Edited by Norman Thomas di Giovanni, Daniel Halpern, and Frank MacShane. New York: E. P. Dutton, 1973. 173 pp. (Paper)
The text of this book is based on tape-recorded transcripts of three meetings that Jorge Luis Borges, a native of Buenos Aires, had with students and faculty of the graduate writing program at Columbia University in the spring of 1971. Each meeting was devoted to a single topic: the writing of fiction, of poetry, and of translation. The Appendix includes an essay on "The Writer's Apprenticeship."

3. Bowen, Elizabeth. "Notes on Writing a Novel,"

in Collected Impressions. London: Longmans, Green and Company, 1950, pp. 249-263. Printed from Orion, II, 1945.

The notes include discussions of plot, characters, scene, dialogue, angle (visual and moral), advance, and relevance.

4. Breit, Harvey. The Writer Observed. New York: Collier Books, 1961. 187 pp.

Short reports of conversations with fifty-nine modern writers about their writing habits as well as Breit's comments on their lives and beliefs. Since the writers were chosen on the basis of their importance as well as on their popular appeal, the list includes both well-established writers and less well-known ones.

5. Buck, Pearl. "Advice to a Novelist about to Be Born, " in Pearl S. Buck. A Biography. Volume Two. Her Philosophy Expressed in Her Letters. By Theodore F. Harris in Consultation with Pearl S. Buck. New York: The John Day Company, 1971, pp. 218-232.

Although she was born in the United States, Pearl S. Buck spent her early years in China as the daughter of missionary parents. The fact that her early writings about China were not readily accepted by publishers provides the basis of her advice to the unborn novelist: Select your own country to be born in and stay there until you leave it of your own will. Do not be born in a foreign country nor spend your childhood there. Above all, avoid being involved by chance of birth and early environment in theological circles. Let your family group be humorous and wayward, gay and intelligent, feeling and sensitive, and let them not care to save their own souls or the souls of others. Never learn to speak a language not your own and begin to speak in the language in which you intend to write.

6. Caldwell, Taylor. "The Essence of Good Writing, " in The Writer's Handbook. Edited by A. S. Burack. Boston: The Writer, Inc., 1967, pp. 21-27.

Caldwell thinks that although writers are born they can also learn certain tricks of the trade. Every writer, she says, should have a liberal arts education, should know at least one language besides his own, and should be a student of the history of man. Since a writer desires to communicate with other men, he must express common experiences or emotions in language that is fresh and has vitality, for only the manner of expression is new, not the ideas. Writing is hard work and a writer knows that he is appreciated when his books are bought and read.

7.   Willa Cather on Writing.   Critical Studies on Writing as an Art.   Foreword by Stephen Tennant.   New York: Alfred A. Knopf, 1949.   126 pp.
Four letters about her work, four critical prefaces, a discussion of Katherine Mansfield's writings, an unpublished fragment, and an essay on "The Art of Fiction" constitute the slim little volume on writing as an art.

8.   Chase, Stuart.   "Writing Nonfiction," in On Writing by Writers.   Edited by William W. West.   New York: Ginn and Company, 1956, pp. 325-330.
Chase discusses eight rules that he offers as guides to the writer of nonfiction prose: select a subject in which you are interested; get some firsthand experience with the subject; decide on your audience; support your generalizations with concrete cases; make an outline before you begin; depart from the outline when necessary; avoid big or fancy words; make notes with care and file them in a logical way.

9.   Chute, B. J.   "When the Writer Comes of Age." The Writer, LXXIX (November, 1966), 20-24.
Chute says that there is no royal road to maturity, for coming of age is a life-time process involving both experience and discipline.   By discipline she means doing one's work even though it may be dull.   One should not be afraid, she says, of rewriting when that is needed, for it is a courtesy due the English language to use it as well as one can. Her first advice to a would-be writer is to read, not "sugar-coated" reading, but the great writers of the past.

10.   Ciardi, John.   "On Writing and Bad Writing," in Dialogue with an Audience.   Philadelphia: J. B. Lippincott, 1963, pp. 262-269.
In a lecture delivered at the opening of the Bread Loaf Writers' Conference, 1962, addressed to the would-be writer, Ciardi says that a writer must be moved to speak his feelings, but that he must also be haunted by language. "Words, sentences, rhythms are not things to him; they are presences.   The presence of his medium makes him feel more than he really knows how to think or say."   He offers several generalizations about writing: the badness of bad writing is never visible to the writer; a writer develops only as rapidly as he learns to recognize what is bad in his writing; the hopeful writer must feel out any criticism for himself.   The writer must be committed to what he is writing but, at the same time, he must be detached, calculating, and technical.   He must be "in the writing," but at

the same time he must have the objective view of an artist outside of it.

11. Ciardi, John. "Work Habits of Writers," in On Writing, By Writers. Edited by William W. West. Boston: Ginn and Company, 1966, pp. 149-155.

"Good writing is rewriting; not merely 'inspired' spillage," says Ciardi. The goal of the writer is to "shape a perception" and to find the language that best suits the perception. Ciardi says that he must have a quiet place in which to write and he seldom finishes a poem at one sitting. He keeps his unfinished poems in a pile and at intervals digs through the pile. If rereading an unfinished poem starts the rhythm again in his head, he can work on the poem again. The last act of writing must be to become one's own reader. "To begin passionately and to end critically, to begin hot and to end cold; and more important, to try to be passion-hot and critic-cold at the same time. For the act of writing a poem is not the act of having an emotion but the act of communicating it."

12. Dunn Elizabeth. "The Writer's Notebook," in The Writer's Handbook. Edited by A. S. Burack. Boston: The Writer, Inc., 1967, pp. 70-76.

Elizabeth Dunn says that notebooks are necessary to prevent details and ideas imbedded in the details from vanishing. A notebook is a place where a writer talks to himself. She says that her notebook is divided into six sections: Conversations, Emotions, Ideas and Plots, Names and Titles, People, Quotations. Drawing on one's notebook "means that one has--very nearly--lived twice: once in the doing, feeling, thinking, and once again in the putting it down on paper."

13. Ellison, Ralph. "Hidden Name and Complex Fate: A Writer's Experience in the United States," in Literary Lectures. Washington, D.C.: Library of Congress, 1973, pp. 552-567.

Ellison says that his experiences as a boy growing up in Oklahoma provided him with raw material for his writing, but that it was through reading that he learned the technique that enabled him to mold his experiences into artistic form. Although he read widely, it is to The Waste Land that he attributes his transition to writing. Later Richard Wright guided him to Henry James's prefaces, to Conrad, to Joseph Warren Beach, and to Dostoievsky. In Harlem he also came in contact with Langston Hughes, who introduced him to the novels of Malraux, who became for Ellison his literary "ancestor."

14. Engle, Paul. "The Writer on Writing," in On Creative Writing. Edited by Paul Engle. New York: E. P. Dutton and Company, Inc., 1966, pp. 3-17. (Paper)

Engle says that there is no such thing as material by itself. The form is part of the content. A writer must develop an intensified perception of life, for the total life of the writer, not just his intuition, is the source of his work. He must also have a high degree of self-knowledge, for it is through the ego that the writer's private events are turned into public forms. Engle thinks that the substance of a writer's work may come from whatever in his observations he recognizes as a part of his own life. The writer can learn further about writing by examining the writing habits of other writers, but always the writer must have control of his own material.

15. Gale, Zona. "Writing as Design," in The Writer and His Craft. Edited by Roy W. Cowden. Ann Arbor: University of Michigan Press, 1956, pp. 30-38. (Paper)

According to Zona Gale, design is the "secret synthesis of art." In fiction, it is the theme treated with heightened awareness. The art of literature, she thinks, is the power to interpret and to communicate values which are incommunicable. Art is another means of apprehension, and design is a way of extending apprehension. It is the business of fiction, therefore, to use its material so that it shows more than appears on the surface.

16. Glasgow, Ellen. "'Preface' to The Sheltered Life," in A Certain Measure, An Interpretation of Prose Fiction. New York: Harcourt, Brace and Company, 1943, pp. 189-210.

This preface is an enlarged version of "One Way to Write Novels," which appeared in The Saturday Review of Literature, December 8, 1934. In this preface, Ellen Glasgow discusses the writing of The Sheltered Life but prefixes the discussion with an explanation of her theories of writing fiction. She suggests that the beginning writer learn the techniques of writing fiction by reading great novels and discussions of the art of fiction, and having thus learned these techniques, try to forget them. She summarizes her method of writing fiction into three rules, the last of which is to endeavor to touch life on every side and at the same time to keep the central vision of the mind "untouched and untouchable."

17. Grau, Shirley Ann. "The Essence of Writing,"
The Writer, LXXXVII (May, 1974), 14-15.
Grau says that a writer is simply one who has developed a facility with words. She believes that writing
cannot be taught but that writing classes are helpful since
peer group pressure forces a beginner to discipline himself
to put something on paper. The life of a writer of fiction,
she says, is a series of "problem-solving experiments in
words," for the goal of all fiction is to make the human
situation understandable to the writer as well as to the
reader.

18. Hemingway, Ernest. "Comments on Writing,"
in Death in the Afternoon. New York: Charles Scribner's
Sons, 1932. Lyceum Edition, pp. 2-3, 54, 191-192.
Hemingway says that he wrote about bullfights because at that time he was trying to learn to write and one
of the simplest things to write about is violent death. This
he found in the bull ring. He warns writers not to confuse
incompetence in writing with mysticism, and not to create
characters in novels but living people, since characters are
only caricatures. He also warns writers against egotism,
especially in showing off knowledge where it does not belong.
"Prose is architecture, not interior decoration, and the
Baroque is over." A good writer, he says, should know
"as near everything as possible." But if a writer of prose
knows enough about what he is writing, he may omit some
things that he knows and the reader will have a feeling of
the things omitted. A writer who omits things he does not
know makes "hollow places in his writing."

19. Hemingway, Ernest. "A Dialogue on Writing,"
in Green Hills of Africa. New York: Charles Scribner's
Sons, 1935. Scribner Library Edition, pp. 2-33.
While hunting kudu in Africa, Hemingway met
Kandisky, a German, with whom he discussed writers and
writing. The discussion is concerned mainly with Hemingway's opinion of American writers. Poe, he says, is a
skillful writer but his writing is dead. Melville is good
but is praised for his rhetoric which is not important.
Emerson, Hawthorne, Whittier had "nice, dry, clean minds,"
but did not use the words of ordinary speech. The good
writers are Henry James, Stephen Crane, and Mark Twain.
"All modern American literature comes from one book by
Mark Twain called Huckleberry Finn.... All American
writing comes from that."

20. Hemingway, Ernest, "Introduction," to In Sicily by Elio Vittorini. Translated by Wilfred Davis. Norfolk, Conn.: New Directions, 1949, pp. 7-9.

Hemingway calls the necessary ingredient for causing dry literature to take on new life rain, which to him means "knowledge, experience, wine, bread, oil, salt, vinegar, bed, early mornings, nights, the sea, men, women, dogs, beloved motor cars, bicycles, hill and valleys, the appearance and disappearance of trains on straight and curved tracks, love, honor, and disobey, music, chamber music and chamber pots, negative and positive Wassermanns, the arrival and non-arrival of expected munitions and/or reinforcements, replacements or your brother. All these are a part of rain to a good writer along with your hated or beloved mother, may she rest in peace or in pieces, porcupine quills, cock grouse drumming on a basswood log, the smell of sweet-grass and fresh smoked leather and Sicily."

21. Highet, Gilbert. "The Final Words," in Explorations. New York: Oxford University Press, 1971, pp. 292-303.

A discussion, with illustrations, of the importance of tone in the concluding sentence of a work. Highet thinks that the final words are more crucial than the first few words since the ending helps to determine the reader's judgment of the work as a whole.

22. Horgan, Paul. Approaches to Writing. Reflections & Notes on the Art of Writing from a Career of Half a Century. New York: Farrar, Straus and Giroux. Noonday Edition, 1974. 233 pp. (Paper)

This book is composed of three parts. Part One, "Talking Shop," consists of comments directed to writers. Part Two is a collection of excerpts from Horgan's notebooks organized under four heads: Process, Of the Mode, Glimpses of the Actual, Behind the Word. Part Three, "Memoir of an Apprentice," is an account of Horgan's own experience as a writer.

23. James, Henry. "The Art of Fiction," in The Art of Fiction and Other Essays. With an Introduction by Morris Roberts. New York: Oxford University Press, 1948, pp. 3-23.

James says that a novel is an organism; in "each of the parts there is something of each of the other parts." His advice to a young writer: "Write from experience only," and "Try to be one of the people upon whom nothing is lost!"

The deepest quality of a work of art will always be the
quality of the producer. "No good novel will ever proceed
from a superficial mind."

24. Janeway, Elizabeth. "The Battle of Fiction and
Non-Fiction," in The Writer's Handbook. Edited by A. S.
Burack. Boston: The Writer, Inc., 1975, pp. 60-65.
Janeway says that non-fiction is more widely read
today than fiction because in our heterogeneous society many
people do not have the kind of background that enables them
as readers to understand and to be moved by the complex
personal relationships presented in many of our novels.
Fiction, she says, should be about recognizable people. The
writer and the reader have to agree that they are talking
about the same facts and the same rules. But the writer
of non-fiction must also be sure that he knows who his audience is. "In more stable times, when people have a better
idea of what's going on around them, they turn to fiction for
an interpretation; whereas, in times like these, people turn
to non-fiction just to find out what's going on."

25. Lees, Hannah. "The Fiction of Non-Fiction,"
in The Writer's Handbook. Edited by A. S. Burack. Boston:
The Writer, Inc., 1967, pp. 322-327.
Hannah Lees, a writer of both fiction and non-fiction,
says that every piece of writing is only as good as the
amount of creative imagination that goes into it, and that the
elements of good non-fiction may be its fictional qualities.
A writer, she says, can decide how he is going to say what
is on his mind only by imagining the impact on his reader.
To provide for understanding, for objectivity, and for avoiding
embarrassment by the use of factual information, the writer
of non-fiction may sometimes have to fictionalize in order to
keep accounts true to life.

26. Maurois, Andre. "The Writer's Craft," in The
Art of Writing. Translated by Gerard Hopkins. New York:
E. P. Dutton and Company, Inc., Dutton Paperback, 1962,
pp. 13-23.
Maurois says that the young writer must first acquire
a vocabulary and master the rules of grammar. The size of
the vocabulary will depend on the nature of the subject, but
clear and simple words of common usage are the best. He
must read the best writers, for from them he can learn the
art of description, of construction, and the use of dialogue,
and from them he will develop a style of his own. He suggests that the writer should never let a day pass without

writing at least a few lines of what he really wants to say,
but writing should not be a substitute for actual experience.

27. Merrill, Paul W. "The Principles of Poor
Writing," Scientific Monthly, LXIV (January, 1947), 72-74.
    A tongue-in-cheek article on the faults of writing.
In order to do a consistently poor job of writing, Merrill
suggests that the student must grasp a few essential principles: ignore the reader, be verbose, vague, and pompous;
fail to revise. He elaborates on each of these principles.

28. O'Connor, Flannery. "The Nature and Aim of
Fiction," in The Writer's Craft. Edited by John Hersey.
New York: Alfred A. Knopf, 1974, pp. 46-56.
    In this lecture to students as part of a course on
"How Writers Write," O'Connor says that the writer of
fiction is interested in what Maritain calls "the habit of
art," or a certain quality or virtue of the mind. She thinks
that the materials of fiction are everything connected with
human beings and that the mistake many writers make is in
trying to be abstract and philosophical. She warns against
naturalism in fiction since in naturalism detail is used because it is natural to life and not natural to art. A fiction
writer must have what she calls "anagogical vision," the
ability to see different levels of reality in one situation.
O'Connor thinks that classes in writing should not attempt
to teach students how to write, but should teach the limits
and possibilities of words and the respect due them. A
teacher's work should be largely negative, to teach students
how not to write. She believes that any discipline in the
curriculum can help with writing, and particularly drawing,
since it helps the writer to look and to see.

29. On Writing, By Writers. Edited by William W.
West. Boston: Ginn and Company, 1966. 417 pp.
    A volume of eleven chapters of material chosen to
represent various phases of contemporary writing and designed to help students form the habit of reading, to interest
them in writing, and to show them how, in literature, structure contributes to meaning. Most of the chapters follow a
definite pattern: an introduction to the individual writer,
representative selections from the author's published works,
the author's original commentary, and two sets of exercises--
for discussion before writing and for writing. The writers
included are Ray Bradbury, Phyllis McGinley, John Updike,
John Ciardi, Paul Gallico, Kay Boyle, Robert Penn Warren,
Lucian Stryk and Hayden Carruth, Stuart Chase, W. Earl

Britton, and Paddy Chayefsky. There is an introductory essay by the editor on the Creative Process.

30. Orwell, George. "Why I Write," in Such, Such Were the Joys. New York: Harcourt, Brace and Company, 1945, pp. 3-11.
Orwell says that a writer's subject matter is determined by the age in which he lives, but that his emotional attitude is acquired at an early age. He discusses four motives that writers have for writing prose: the desire to seem clever, egoism; pleasure in good writing, the aesthetic motive; the desire to see and to present things as they are, the historical impulse; the desire to change society, the political purpose.

31. Porter, Katherine Anne. "Three Statements about Writing," in The Days Before. Freeport, N.Y.: Books for Libraries Press, 1971, pp. 123-132.
The statements are organized under three heads: "1939: The Situation in American Writing"; "1940: Introduction to Flowering Judas"; and "1942: Transplanted Writers." In the first section, Porter answers seven questions about her own writing; in the second version, written seven days after the fall of France, she shows her concern for the future of art and of mankind in general; in the third section, she replies to the question as to the harm done by the displacement of world writers by saying that the old quarrels and old prejudices of Europe have brought catastrophe upon all of us, and she agrees with E. M. Forster that the only two possibilities for real order are in art and in religion.

32. Roberts, Kenneth. I Wanted to Write. Garden City, N.Y.: Doubleday and Company, Inc., 1949. 471 pp.
An autobiographical account of how Kenneth Roberts, who knew that he wanted to write while still a college student, made a living mainly by writing articles for the Saturday Evening Post while planning, doing the research, and writing seven novels in addition to numerous shorter articles. Throughout the book, he points out the toil and frustrations as well as the satisfaction of a writer's life.

33. Seton, Anya. "The Writer's Requisites," The Writer, LXXX (August, 1967), 19, 45.
A true writer, says Seton, must continue to write in spite of setbacks. She believes that the two keys to unlocking the doors to success in writing are constant attention

and perseverance, and she suggests that the best way to sustain these requisites is through reading and study. She urges writers to rewrite constantly and to listen as they write. "Remember that words were audible long before arbitrary symbols made them visual to us."

34. Shedd, Margaret. "Writing Techniques and Freedom," The Writer, LXXXI (May, 1968); 13-15.
People write for many reasons, says Margaret Shedd, but there is one kind of writer who writes because he wants the freedom that he finds only in the creation of a world that is more bearable than the real one. "There is no freedom in writing without the absolute need to write and without the learning of appropriate skills, and these two mutual demands will forever generate creative forces." She believes that the intuition of the writer is important but that writing skills can be acquired only by putting words down on paper. Thus the writer finds that technique provides him with the passport to writing freedom.

35. Stafford, Jean. "Wordman, Spare That Tree!" Saturday Review/World, July 13, 1974, pp. 14-17.
Stafford believes that writing can be learned through practice and that analysis of writing helps the student to know better what writing is and therefore adds to his enjoyment of reading. In addition to having talent, the writer must have drive, the ability to accept failure, the need to write, and the hope for excellence.

36. Stark, Freya. "Saying What One Means," Atlantic Monthly, CCXII (October, 1963), 102-103.
Freya Stark says that the basis of style is accuracy, having the capacity to say more or less what one means. The problem of all writing is to convey a meaning with the use of few and always inadequate words, combined with what the reader, drawing upon his own reserves, will understand. "The number of words that even the most profuse writer will dare to use is always insufficient for a complete impression, but the reserves that he can draw upon in the reader's mind are lavish indeed."

37. To the Young Writer. Hopwood Lectures, Second Series. Edited by A. L. Bader. Ann Arbor: University of Michigan Press, 1965. 196 pp. (Paper)
The Hopwood Lectures are given at the University of Michigan on the occasion of the presentation of the Avery Hopwood and Jule Hopwood Awards in Creative Writing. This

volume, concerned with various topics related to writing,
consists of twelve lectures delivered from 1953 through 1964.
The speakers are Stephen Spender, John Gassner, Archibald
MacLeish, Philip Rahv, Malcolm Cowley, John Ciardi, Howard
Nemerov, Theodore Roethke, Saul Bellow, Mark Schorer,
Arthur Miller, and Alfred Kazin.

      38. Welty, Eudora. "How I Write," Virginia Quar-
terly Review, XXXI (Spring, 1955), 240-251.
      Eudora Welty says that place is important in her
writing. "In a way place is your honor as it is your wisdom,
and would make you responsible to it for what you put down
for the truth." She thinks that criticism can be an art, but
the writing of a story and a criticism of it go in opposite directions. She illustrates her comments by referring to the
writing of one of her own stories.

      39. Welty, Eudora. "Place in Fiction," The South
Atlantic Quarterly, LV (January, 1956), 57-72.
      In this essay, Welty continues her discussion of place
with particular reference to the contribution of place to
"goodness" in the novel. This "goodness" she considers
from three aspects: the raw material of writing; the writing
itself; the writer himself, for place is where he has roots
and where he gains his experience. Miss Welty objects to
the term "regional" since it fails "to differentiate between
the localized raw material of life and its outcome as art."
Place, she says, not only furnishes "a plausible abode" for
the novel's world of feeling but helps to make the characters
real, for by limiting his world the character is defined.
"Place in fiction is the named, identified, concrete, exact
and exacting, and therefore credible, gathering-spot of all
that has been felt, is about to be experienced, in the novel's
progress."

      40. Welty, Eudora. "Some Notes on Time in Fic-
tion," Mississippi Quarterly, XXVI (Fall, 1973), 483-492.
      Welty says that time and place must operate together
in the novel, yet the novelist lives on closer terms with
time than with place, for time is involved in the plot, especially in suspense, and is the mover of action. Time un-
covers motives and develops the consequences. Time acts
as a resolver. Fiction can accelerate time, slow it down,
or have it run forward or backward. "Time in a novel is
the course through which, and by which, all things in their
turn are brought forth in their significance--events, emotions,
relationships in the changes, in their synchronized move

toward resolution. It provides the order for the dramatic
unfolding of the plot; revelation is not revelation until it is
dramatically conceived and carried out."

41. Welty, Eudora. "Words into Fiction," The
Southern Review, I, n.s. (July, 1965), 543-553.
    Welty says that learning to write may be a part of
learning to read, but writing fiction cannot be learned from
copying out of books. How to write is not concerned with
the abstract, but with the specific in the work at hand. Experience, the raw material of fiction, must be acted upon by
the novelist, for it is nothing without his interpretation. The
experience of the reader provides an added dimension, for
the reader, through what the writer suggests, sees a distance
beyond what the writer actually says. The finished novel, although highly personal, is still objective, and it is in the
ways that prose achieves its objectivity that the writer has
style. But Welty goes beyond style to what she calls shape,
which to her is something "felt" as one writes, and as one
reads "it tells over the whole, as a whole to the reader's
memory." To the reader shape is the aesthetic pattern he
sees in the novel; to the writer shape is closely related to
the course of the work itself.

42. Wharton, Edith. "Confessions of a Novelist,"
Atlantic Monthly CLI (April, 1933), 385-392.
    Edith Wharton says that sometimes the situation of a
novel occurs first in her mind and sometimes the characters
appear first. The characters always have names and sometimes names appear without the characters. The characters
provide the dialogue and she sets down only what the characters say, but from the first she knows what is going to happen to them and all that she does is to watch and record.
There are only two essential rules for choosing material for
a novel: what is within the writer's reach and what the
writer sees in it. Real people cannot be used in a work of
fiction, for only those born of the creator's brain can give
the illusion of reality.

43. Woolf, Virginia. "Craftsmanship," in Collected
Essays. New York: Harcourt, Brace and World, Inc.,
1966, II, 245-251.
    In a broadcast on April 20, 1937, Virginia Woolf dis-
cusses two qualities of words: their inability to convey
exact meaning and their power to tell the truth. Words,
she says, are so filled with associations, with memories,
that they cannot be impersonal and their use cannot be taught

for "they live in the mind." "They hate being useful; they hate making money; they hate being lectured about in public. In short, they hate anything that stamps them with one meaning or confines them to one attitude, for it is their nature to change."

44. Woolf, Virginia. A Room of One's Own. New York: Harcourt, Brace and World, Inc., 1957. 118 pp. (Paper)
This essay is based on two papers that Virginia Woolf read to the Arts Society at Newnham and the Odtaa at Girton in October, 1928. She gives a survey of the positions of women throughout the centuries, positions which show that women have not been given the opportunity by education, by social position, and by economic security to become writers. Her conclusion is that a woman must have the freedom provided by money and a room of her own if she is to write fiction.

45. The Writer's Craft. Edited by John Hersey. New York: Alfred A. Knopf, 1974. 425 pp.
A collection of essays in seven parts. The essays are concerned with the aims of art, the question of method, the relation of language to writing and to politics, the writing process, the writer's life, and the writing itself. In addition to an introduction by the editor, there is a short list of books and of essays on writing by accomplished writers.

46. Writers on Writing. Compiled and edited by Walter Allen. New York: E. P. Dutton and Company, Inc., 1959. 358 pp. (Paper)
A collection of notes, critical statements, extracts from letters, and extracts from their writing of important poets and novelists, "eminent practitioners" of the art of writing. Accounts of how specific works originated and were written are also included. The material was selected with the idea of making a book that would help the young writer.

47. "The Writing of Nonfiction Prose," in Teaching Creative Writing. Washington, D.C.: Library of Congress, 1974, pp. 94-131. (Paper)
The Conference on Teaching Creative Writing, January 29-30, 1973, at the Library of Congress, had as members of the panel for nonfiction prose the following writers: John Ciardi, chairman; Ralph Ellison; Josephine Jacobsen; William J. Lederer; N. Scott Momaday; Luis D. Rubin, Jr.; and Wallace Stegner. The comments by the members of this

panel relate particularly to the similarities between fiction and nonfiction. Ciardi defines nonfiction as "what becomes of a body of information when it falls into the hands of a man who would like to write a novel (or a short story) but who lacks faith in the scope of his emotion, or who suspects he couldn't sell the stuff if he made fiction of it." Ellison stresses the importance of fact in nonfiction and in fiction the force of the human will.

WRITING ASSIGNMENTS

1. Read the selections by Frost in Robert Frost on Writing and write a paper in which you present in well-organized form what Frost has to say about writing.

2. Pearl S. Buck advises novelists to learn to speak in the language in which they intend to write. Yet Joseph Conrad, from Poland, wrote novels in English. Write a paper in which you discuss some of the problems that a writer encounters in writing in a language not his native language. You may want to examine a story or novel by Conrad to see if you can determine some of his difficulties. You may also want to read A Personal Record as well as some of his critical essays.

3. George Orwell says that the starting point of much of his writing in the last ten years was to present an injustice, to expose a falsehood, to draw attention to a political situation, but that he was always conscious of prose style and that it was when he lacked a political purpose that he wrote lifeless books. Do you agree that propagandistic literature may also be artistic? Select a political novel that you know and write a paper in which you discuss the relation of the political motive to the artistic accomplishment, if any. You may want to use one of the following novels: Henry Adams, Democracy, 1880; Günter Grass, The Tin Drum, 1959; Arthur Koestler, Darkness at Noon, 1941; Adria Locke Langley, A Lion in the Streets, 1945; Sinclair Lewis, It Can't Happen Here, 1935; George Orwell, Nineteen Eighty-Four, 1959; Ignazio Silone, Bread and Wine, 1937; Robert Penn Warren, All the King's Men, 1946.

4. Highet comments on the fact that some writers such as Gibbon and Tolstoy detract from their works by concluding with personal notes or with material not directly related to the work itself. Write a paper in which you discuss

both good and bad endings of works that you know. You
may use any of the forms of writing.

5. Taylor Caldwell says that a would-be writer should
have a liberal arts education, should know at least one language besides his own, and should be a student of the history
of man. Write a paper in which you comment on her statement and present your views of the kind of preparation a
person who plans to make his living by writing should have.
What should be the preparation in college of a student who
wants to write acceptable prose?

6. In "The Writing of Nonfiction Prose," William J.
Lederer tells how he and Eugene Burdick, the authors of The
Ugly American (1958), decided a short time before the book
was to be published that it must be changed from a factual
account to fiction since the readers would believe it more as
fiction. They burned the 31 copies of the manuscript and in
six days rewrote the book. Read The Ugly American, including "A Factual Epilogue," and write a paper in which you
discuss the differences in fiction and nonfiction and point out
the changes you think Lederer and Burdick had to make to
change the book to fiction. Before you begin, read "The
Fiction of Non-Fiction" by Hannah Lees and "The Battle of
Fiction and Non-Fiction" by Elizabeth Janeway.

INTERVIEWS WITH WRITERS

The ideas of modern writers on such topics as the sources of their material, their methods of writing, the influence of other writers on their writing, their use of language, etc., are of interest to the student of writing since they provide insights into how accomplished writers perform, information about the knowledge and the discipline required of the writer, and stimulation to the student in his own writing. Many of the writers interviewed express similar ideas, but their accounts show that there is no one best way to learn to write and that talents and interests must be developed. In these interviews the writers reveal their ideas and techniques candidly and seriously, for as Alfred Kazin says of The Paris Review Interviews, "no proper writer can afford to lie in an interview of this type." There are drawbacks, however. A writer may have forgotten exactly what happened when he wrote a particular piece, or he may be asked questions about topics in which he has little knowledge or interest. But in the main, the interviews not only provide information about writing; they introduce the students to the backgrounds and personalities of the writers themselves. Writers become human beings who have struggled just as the student is struggling, and writing becomes the link between the inexperienced and the accomplished writers.

Interviews with Writers (Collections)

1. African Writers Talking. A Collection of Radio Interviews. Edited by Dennis Duerden and Cosmo Pieterse. New York: African Publishing Corporation, 1972. 195 pp. (Paper)
   These interviews were originally produced, over a period of six years, on African radio by the Transcription Center, London. Eighteen English-speaking writers give first-hand accounts of the development of post-Independence

African literature. The writers were asked such questions as "What is African writing? How do you write? Why do you write about particular things? How do you feel about such topics as negritude and the writer as teacher?" The writers talk about their own work and the relation of their writing to the African audience.

2. The Contemporary Writer. Interviews with Sixteen Novelists and Poets. Edited by L. S. Dembo and Cyrena N. Pondrom. Madison: University of Wisconsin Press, 1972. 296 pp. (Paper)
These interviews with eight novelists and eight poets for Contemporary Literature were held over a period of six years (March 20, 1964-September 9, 1970) and were first published in the journal. They are concerned not only with the technicalities of writing but also with the writer's philosophic, ethical, and aesthetic opinions. The novelists are John Hawkes, John Barth, Saul Bellow, Vladimir Nabokov, Isaac Bashevis Singer, Jorge Luis Borges, Sara Lidman, and Per Olaf Sundman. The poets are James Merrill, Kenneth Rexroth, George Oppen, Carl Rakosi, Charles Reznikoff, Louis Zukofsky, Gwendolyn Brooks, and George Barker.

3. Conversations. By Roy Newquist. Chicago: Rand McNally and Company, 1967. 505 pp.
Several writers, editors, critics, and publishers, representative of various "levels" of writing, are interviewed by Newquist, literary editor of Chicago's American. In addition, there are eleven vignettes adapted from their initial appearance in Chicago's American. The long list of writers includes Arnold Toynbee, Robert St. John, Ogden Nash, James Michener, Katherine Anne Porter, Robert Penn Warren, Will and Ariel Durant, Irving Wallace, Christopher Isherwood, and Lerone Bennett, Jr.

4. First Person. Conversations on Writers and Writing with Glenway Westcott, John Dos Passos, Robert Penn Warren, John Updike, John Barth, Robert Coover. Edited by Frank Gado. Schenectady, N.Y.: Union College Press, 1973. 159 pp.
Interviews in which a group of Union College faculty and students met informally with the authors. A long introduction by the editor provides background for the conversations and for the writers, who extend over fifty years of American fiction and in general represent each decade since the First World War.

5. Interviews with Black Writers. Edited by John
O'Brien. New York: Liveright, 1973. 274 pp.
    Interviews with seventeen Black Writers with an intro-
duction by the editor on the development of the black literary
tradition. The writers are Arna Bontemps, Cyrus Colter,
William Demby, Owen Dodson, Ralph Ellison, Ernest J.
Gaines, Michael Harper, Robert Hayden, Clarence Major,
Julian Mayfield, Ann Petry, Ishmael Reed, Alice Walker,
John Wideman, John Williams, Charles Wright, and Al Young.

6. Kite-Flying and Other Irrational Acts. Conversations with Twelve Southern Writers. Edited by John Carr.
Baton Rouge: Louisiana State University Press, 1972.
288 pp.
    All of the writers included in this volume are white;
every writer has just completed a book; all talk about
writing in general; two are also writers of nonfiction; one
is a woman. Except for part of one interview, all interviews took place April 1969-October 1971. The writers are
Shelby Foote, Walker Percy, Marion Montgomery, Reynolds
Price, Willie Morris, Larry E. King, Doris Betts, George
Garrett, Jesse Hill Ford, Fred Chappell, Guy Owen, and
James Whitehead.

7. The Paris Review, Writers at Work: The Paris
Review Interviews, First Series, edited, with an introduction by Malcolm Cowley, 1958; Second Series, edited by
George Plimpton, with an introduction by Van Wyck Brooks,
1963; Third Series, edited by George Plimpton, with an in-
troduction by Alfred Kazin, 1967. New York: The Viking
Press.
    In the First Series, in addition to interviews by
various reporters with sixteen novelists, Cowley has an in-
troductory essay on "How Writers Write." The writers are
Francois Mauriac, E. M. Forster, Joyce Cary, Dorothy
Parker, James Thurber, Thornton Wilder, William Faulkner,
Georges Simenon, Frank O'Connor, Robert Penn Warren,
Alberto Moravia, Nelson Algren, Angus Wilson, William
Styron, Truman Capote, and Francoise Sagan. The Second
Series includes several kinds of writers--poets, essayists,
novelists, humorists--from various places. The fourteen
writers talk about when they write, on teaching and writing,
and on their own experiences. Only Robert Lowell talks
about technique. The other writers are Boris Pasternak,
T. S. Eliot, Ernest Hemingway, Marianne Moore, Ralph
Ellison, Robert Frost, S. J. Perelman, Lawrence Durrell,
Mary McCarthy, Aldous Huxley, Ezra Pound, Henry Miller,

and Katherine Anne Porter. The Third Series includes in-
terviews with fourteen writers: William Carlos Williams,
Blaise Cendrars, Jean Cocteau, Louis-Ferdinand Céline,
Evelyn Waugh, Lillian Hellman, William Burroughs, Saul
Bellow, Arthur Miller, James Jones, Norman Mailer, Allen
Ginsberg, Edward Albee, and Harold Pinter.

8. The Poet Speaks. Interviews with Contemporary
Poets Conducted by Hilary Morrish, Peter Orr, John Press,
and Ian Scott-Kilvert. General Editor, Peter Orr. Preface
by Frank Kermode. New York: Barnes and Noble, Inc.,
1966. 276 pp.
    Interviews with forty-five modern poets. Included are
such well-known poets as Edmund Blunden, Roy Fuller, David
Jones, Sylvia Plath, Herbert Read, and Stephen Spender. The
questions concern mainly how the poet began writing, the relation of poetry to other arts, how and when one writes, the
audience for which poets write, and their views of contemporary poems.

9. Writers and Writing. Edited by Robert Van
Gelder. New York: Charles Scribner's Sons, 1946. 381 pp.
    A series of interviews with more than a hundred
writers--novelists, biographers, historians, detective-story
writers, etc.--American as well as British and European.
The interviews begin in 1940 with H. L. Mencken and end
in 1946 with Erich Remarque. A long introduction summarizes the attitudes and experiences of the writers interviewed.

Interviews with Individual Writers

1. Borges, Jorge Luis. Interview in The Contemporary Writer. Interviews with Sixteen Novelists and Poets.
Edited by L. S. Dembo and Cyrene N. Pondrom. Madison:
University of Wisconsin Press, 1972, pp. 113-121.
    The interview, held in English, was conducted in
Madison, Wisconsin, November 21, 1969. Borges describes
himself as an idealist and discusses his use of symbols, especially the image of the labyrinth that is used throughout
his writing.

2. Conversations with Jorge Luis Borges by Richard
Burgin. New York: Holt, Rinehart and Winston, 1968,
1969. 144 pp.
    During the 1967-1968 academic year Borges was
Charles Eliot Norton Professor at Harvard. These interviews

were conducted during the year by Richard Burgin, a student
at Brandeis University who also attended some of Borges's
lectures at Harvard.

3. "The Art of Fiction: Jorge Luis Borges," Inter-
view with Ronald Christ, Paris Review, No. 40 (Winter-
Spring, 1967), 116-164.
Borges explains how he began to write fiction.

4. Brooks, Gwendolyn. Interview with Paul M.
Angle (Illinois Bell Interviews), Summer, 1967, in Gwendolyn
Brooks, Report from Part One. Prefaces by Don L. Lee
and George Kent. Detroit: Broadside Press, 1972, pp.
131-146.
In this interview Gwendolyn Brooks says that encouragement for writing should begin with the very young and that
fellowships for writers should be provided. She thinks that a
writer should get as much education as possible and that he
must read "almost more than his eyes can bear," not only in
his own field but in related fields. He needs to write and to
"live richly with eyes open, and heart, too."

5. Brooks, Gwendolyn. Interview with George Stav-
ros, March 28, 1969, in Report from Part One, pp. 147-
166. Also included in The Contemporary Writer, pp. 233-252.
A conversation about Brooks's ideas of poetry as an
art and of the work of other contemporary black poets.

6. Brooks, Gwendolyn. Interview with Ida Lewis
(Essence Magazine Interviews), Spring, 1971, in Report from
Part One, pp. 167-182.
Mainly an account of Brooks's development as a poet.

7. Ellison, Ralph. "The Art of Fiction: An Inter-
view," in Writers at Work. The Paris Review Interviews.
Second series. Introduction by Van Wyck Brooks. New
York: The Viking Press, 1963, pp. 320-334. Originally
published in The Paris Review, No. 8 (Spring, 1955), 54-71.
Reprinted in Shadow and Act, 1964, pp. 167-183.
The interview by Alfred Chester and Vilma Howard
was held in Paris on the day before Ellison was to return to
the United States after a year in Europe. In the interview,
Ellison is concerned particularly with art and with the novel.
He thinks that the universal in the novel is reached only
through the representation of a specific person in a specific
circumstance. He says that both the Negro novelist and the
white reader are too much aware of themselves when they
write and when they read. "The understanding of art depends

finally upon one's willingness to extend one's humanity and one's knowledge of human life." Negro folklore, he says, is important to the Negro novelist, for it shows that he trusts his own experiences and sensibilities. He says that the changes in style in Invisible Man express both the hero's state of consciousness and the state of society. He believes that one function of serious literature is to deal with the moral core of a given society and that his novel has contributed to the shaping of our culture as he would like it to be.

8. Ellison, Ralph. "A Very Stern Discipline. An Interview with Ralph Ellison," Harper's Magazine, CCXXXIV (March, 1967), 76-95.
The interviewers were three young Negro writers, James Thompson, Lennox Raphael, and Steve Cannon. The questions are concerned mainly with the Negro writer and his situation in America as compared with that of the Jewish writer, Ellison's opinions of other writers, the responsibility of the Negro writer to civil rights and to American literature as a whole, and the political pressures on the Negro writer. Ellison advises the young writer to realize that writing is "a very stern discipline," to read many good books in the literary form he expects to use, to educate himself as well as he can, and to use his imagination to penetrate the surface of society.

9. Stern, Richard G. "An Interview with Ralph Ellison," in Black Voices. Edited, with an Introduction and Biographical Notes, by Abraham Chapman. New York: The New American Library. Mentor Books, 1968, pp. 645-649. (Paper) Published originally in the Chicago Literary magazine december, III (Winter, 1961), 30-32, under the title "That Same Pain, That Same Pleasure." Included in Ellison's Shadow and Act, 1964, pp. 23-41.
In this interview Ellison discusses the limitations and the advantages of growing up as a Negro in Oklahoma, his interest in music, and the encouragement to write that he received from Richard Wright. He says that what he has tried to commemorate in fiction is "that which I believe to be enduring and abiding in our situation, especially those human qualities which the American Negro has developed despite and in rejection of the obstacles and meannesses imposed upon us. If the writer exists for any social good, his role is that of preserving in art those human values which can endure by confronting change." Writing, he says, is his way of confronting both pain and pleasure and of seeing that it is not all in vain.

10. Ellison, Ralph. "A Completion of Personality," in The Writer's Craft. Edited by John Hersey. New York: Alfred A. Knopf, 1974, pp. 276-282. Also in Ralph Ellison: Collection of Critical Essays. Edited by John Hersey. Englewood Cliffs, N. J.: Prentice-Hall, 1974, pp. 1-19.

In this interview with John Hersey, Ellison tells of the influence of his father who wanted him to be a poet and of his mother who interested him in reading, in helping him to understand people, and in providing him with an awareness of political conditions. Ellison talks about writing Invisible Man; about how he writes and his relations to his characters; the ways in which his musical experience has affected his writing; the reader for whom he writes; the influence on his writing of Joyce, Dostoievsky, and Tolstoy; and the background of the Negro American writer as fictional material.

11. Bouvard, Loïc. "Conversations with William Faulkner," Modern Fiction Studies, V (Winter, 1959-1960), 361-364. Translation from the French by Henry Dan Piper. Interview appeared originally in Bulletin de l'association amicale universitaire France-Amérique, January, 1954, pp. 23-29. Included in Lion in the Garden, pp. 68-73.

The interview took place at Princeton Inn, on November 30, 1952, when Bouvard, a native of France, was a student at Princeton University. The conversation is concerned mainly with philosophical and moral matters--God, man, time, art. "Art," says Faulkner, "is not only man's most supreme expression; it is also the salvation of mankind." Faulkner agrees that writing is hard work. "A great book is always accompanied by a painful birth." He mentions Flaubert, Balzac, Bergson, and Proust as having influenced his writing.

12. Faulkner at Nagano. Edited by Robert A. Jelliffe. Tokyo: Kenkyusha Ltd., 1956. 206 pp.

In August, 1955, Faulkner went to Japan at the invitation of the United States Department of State to take part in the Nagano Seminar. In addition to talks and interviews with members of this group, he also spoke on various other occasions and answered questions on many topics including questions on his own writing.

13. Faulkner at West Point. Edited by Joseph L. Fant, III, and Robert Ashley, with the Assistance of Other Members of the English Department, United States Military Academy. New York: Random House, 1964. 136 pp.

This is a record of Faulkner's visit to West Point in April, 1962. Except for a reading from his works at the University of Virginia on May 17 and a visit to New York City on May 24 to accept the Gold Medal of the National Institute of Arts and Letters, the West Point visit was Faulkner's last public appearance. In addition to reading from The Reivers, Faulkner answered questions during a Press Conference as well as in sessions with cadets in classes in American literature. Many of the questions relate to Faulkner's own writing.

14. Faulkner in the University. Class Conferences at the University, 1957-1958. Edited by Frederick L. Gwynn and Joseph L. Blotner. New York: Alfred A. Knopf, Inc., 1965. Copyright by the University of Virginia Press, 1959. Vintage Edition. 295 pp. (Paper)
Faulkner was Writer-in-Residence at the University of Virginia from February to June of 1957 and 1958. During this time he held thirty-seven group conferences as well as a number of individual meetings with students and members of the staff of the University. Thirty-six of the sessions are here reproduced. The questions are largely concerned with the problems of writing and of the South.

15. Lion in the Garden: Interviews with William Faulkner, 1926-1962. Edited by James B. Meriwether and Michael Millgate. New York: Rnadom House, 1968. 298 pp.
This is a collection of significant interviews, both in the United States and abroad, from the beginning to the end of Faulkner's career. This collection supplements the interviews and classroom discussions at the University of Virginia and at West Point and includes the texts of the Nagano Seminars. The interviews are arranged in chronological order according to the date of the interview. A valuable index provides references to Faulkner's works, his references to other writers, and references to the themes of his writing.

16. Ciardi, John. "An Interview with Robert Frost," in Dialogue with an Audience. Boston: J. B. Lippincott Company, 1963, pp. 169-178.
The conversation took place on March 21, 1959, in Frost's winter home in Miami, Florida. The interview began with Frost's talking about his forthcoming book, which led into a discussion of poetry and the poet. "A poem," he says, "is a momentary stay against confusion ... an arrest of disorder." Frost also talks about his work as a Consultant in Poetry at the Library of Congress and as a teacher and lecturer in various colleges.

17. Frost, A Time to Talk. Conversations and Indiscretions Recorded by Robert Francis. Amherst: University of Massachusetts, 1972. 100 pp.

These conversations are given in two sections: 1950-1959 and 1933-1935. The "Epilogue" includes an account of Frost's eightieth birthday dinner, an account of "The Robert Frost Memorial Service," and of "Frost Today," Francis's assessment of Frost. Francis, a neighbor of Frost, was a teacher of English in the high school at Amherst for one year. He first met Frost in January, 1933.

18. Interviews with Robert Frost. Edited by Edward Connery Lathem. New York: Holt, Rinehart and Winston, 1966. 295 pp.

A selection of interviews that extend from 1915, the year Robert Frost returned to the United States from England, through 1962, just a few weeks before his death. The interviews are arranged in chronological order and are divided into six sections by decades. All are from printed sources and include newspaper accounts of his interviews. Of these three are Russian newspaper accounts of his trip to Russia.

19. Borach, Georges. "Conversations with James Joyce," College English, XV (March, 1954), 325-327. Translated from Neue Zurcher Zeitung of May 3, 1931, by Joseph Prescott.

These are notes of conversations with James Joyce in Zurich, on August 1, 1917, November 15, 1917, October 21, 1918, and June 18, 1919, by Georges Borach, one of Joyce's language students in Zurich. At this time Joyce was working on Ulysses and his comments are concerned with the Odyssey and with how he came to write Ulysses. He says that the theme of the Odyssey is the "most beautiful" and the subject of Odysseus the most human in world literature.

20. Morris, Willie. "Down Home," in Kite-Flying and Other Irrational Acts. Conversations with Twelve Southern Writers. Edited by John Carr. Baton Rouge: Louisiana State University Press, 1972, pp. 96-119.

Morris says that one of the reasons that the South has produced so many writers is that Southerners grow up with words, with the telling of tales. Southern writers, he says, carry the burden of memory and it is very important that a Southern writer keep in close touch with his home, for he both loves it and hates it. He thinks that nonfiction forms of writing are better than they have ever been.

21. Lanier, Doris. "Mary Noailles Murfree: An Interview," Tennessee Historical Quarterly, XXI (Fall, 1972), 276-278. Reproduction of an article from the Macon (Georgia) Telegraph, November 15, 1895.
This is a report of an interview (interviewer not identified) with Joseph A. Farrell, who spent three weeks at Montvale Springs, in East Tennessee, while Mary Noailles Murfree was staying there and working on The Prophet of the Great Smoky Mountains. Farrell comments on Miss Murfree's personal characteristics and her habits of work. He says that, according to her statements, she was well paid for her writing.

22. "An Interview with Vladimir Nabokov," in Nabokov: The Man and His Work. Edited by L. S. Dembo. Madison: University of Wisconsin Press, 1967, pp. 19-44. Originally published in Wisconsin Studies in Contemporary Literature, VII, No. 2 (Spring, 1967).
The interview was conducted by Alfred Appel, Jr., on September 25, 27, 28, 29, 1966, in Nabokov's home in Montreux, Switzerland. The interviewer was a student of Nabokov at Cornell University in 1954. In the interview, Nabokov gives his opinions of American writers, of Freud, and of the value of criticism. He describes his method of writing as very slow and with much rewriting. He says that at the beginning of a work he has a "curiously clear preview of the entire novel." The entire book seems to be ready and his job is "to take down as much of it as I can make out and as precisely as I am humanly able to." In referring to the gulf between the two cultures, Nabokov says, "There is no science without fancy and no art without facts."

23. Nabokov, Vladimir. "Interviews," in Strong Opinions. New York: McGraw-Hill Book Company, 1973, pp. 1-207.
The twenty-two interviews included in this section extend from June 5, 1962, to October, 1972. They include four television interviews, two British and two American, and interviews for newspapers and magazines, both in the United States and abroad. The questions for the interviews were sent to Nabokov in writing and were answered in writing. Thus the interviews give Nabokov's considered opinions and not his spontaneous reactions.

24. "An Interview with Flannery O'Connor and Robert Penn Warren," held at the Vanderbilt Literary Symposium, April 23, 1959, in Writer to Writers: Readings on the Craft

of Writing. Edited by Floyd C. Watkins and Karl F. Knight.
Boston: Houghton Mifflin Company, 1966, pp. 71-90. (Paper)
Reprinted from The Vagabond, Vanderbilt University, 1960.
The interview was edited by Cyrus Hoy and Walter Sullivan.
Other participants were Joe Sills, Jr., Edwin Godsey, Randall
Mize, Harry Minetree, Jim Whitehead, Bill Harrison, Tom
McNair, Betty Weber, Walter Russell, George Core, and
Chris Boner.

Many of the questions concern procedures for writing
stories and novels. Warren answers questions about All the
King's Men and Brother to Dragons. O'Connor discusses the
use of the grotesque in her writing. Both writers give their
opinions about the South as a literary region. Warren says
that when one sits down to write he has to forget critical
thinking.

25. Porter, Katherine Anne. Interview in Writers
at Work. The Paris Review Interviews, Second Series. Introduction by Van Wyck Brooks. New York: The Viking
Press, Compass Books Edition, 1963, pp. 137-163.

The interview by Barbara Thompson took place in the
home of Katherine Anne Porter. Miss Porter talks about
how she started writing, the books and writers that influenced
her, her family ties, her work for a newspaper, her struggle
to write, her flight to Mexico, and her experience with the
Mexican revolution. She thinks that art is a vocation and to
follow it one must sometimes lead a kind of monastic life.
She says that she always writes the ending of a story first
and then works towards that. She always writes a story at
one sitting, but she worked at intervals for twenty years on
Ship of Fools. She believes that there is a basic pure human
speech in every language and that you can't use jargon in
writing about people and you cannot write out of textbooks.

26. "An Interview with Wallace Stegner," in Fiction
and Analysis: Seven Major Themes. Edited by Robert
Canzoni and Page Stegner. Glenview, Illinois: Scott, Foresman and Company, 1970, pp. 123-127.

The interview is concerned with Stegner's writing of
the short story "Genesis," but it also includes discussions as
to whether a writer writes from theme, situation, or character, and whether a writer relies on the facts of experience
or allows his imagination to operate in a given situation.
Stegner says that fiction should reflect actual life but that
sometimes facts have to bend in order to reflect a situation
realistically.

27. "The Art of Fiction XVIII: Robert Penn Warren,"
in Writers at Work. The Paris Review Interviews, First
Series. Edited by Malcolm Cowley. New York: The Viking
Press, Inc., Compass Books Edition, 1959, pp. 183-207.
Included in Robert Penn Warren: A Collection of Critical
Essays. Edited by John Lewis Longley, Jr. N.Y.: New
York University Press, 1965, pp. 18-45. Originally published
in Paris Review, IV (Spring-Summer, 1957).
    The interview by Ralph Ellison and Eugene Walter took
place in the apartment of Ellison at the American Academy in
Rome. Warren talks about his early reading, his attitudes
toward criticism, his interest in the craft of other writers,
and his ideas of freedom for the individual in conduct and in
personal life. He says that he tries to forget abstractions
when he is composing and he has no patience with "experi-
mental writing," for writing is for keeps. He says that his
novels are not historical but an awareness of history is always present. He mentions his relation to the Fugitive
Group and the effect the members of the group had on his
writing. He thinks that there is a parallel between New
England before the Civil War and the South after World War I
in that in each place a cultural shock caused an intellectual
ferment in a more or less static society.

28. Bunting, Charles T. "The Interior World: An
Interview with Eudora Welty," The Southern Review, VII
(October, 1972), 711-735.
    The interview took place in Welty's home in Jackson,
Mississippi, on January 24, 1972. Welty talks about the
people who helped her get her first writing published, the
writing of The Golden Apples, and her work with students.
She does not believe in teaching writing, but having students
write and talk about what they have written is helpful. She
thinks that since writing starts from an internal feeling, the
analysis of another writer's form does not really help a
writer. She reads Jane Austen, E. M. Forster, Henry
Green, Virginia Woolf, and such critics as Edmund Wilson
and Robert Penn Warren, but she says that comments on her
writing are of little value to her.

29. "The Southern Imagination: An Interview with
Eudora Welty and Walker Percy," Mississippi Quarterly,
XXVI (Fall, 1973), 493-516. By William F. Buckley, Jr.
A reprint of the transcript of the Firing Line television pro-
gram conducted by William F. Buckley, Jr., and taped at
WMAA in Jackson, Mississippi, December 12, 1972. The
panelists are Gordon Weaver, Jerry Ward, and Dan Hise.

The discussion is concerned mainly with the work of Southern writers, their attitudes and peculiar characteristics, the effect of the Civil War and the race situation on their writing, the relation of Southern writers to writers in other parts of the country, the loss of Southern tradition, and the contributions of Southern writers to American culture as a whole.

30. White, Theodore H. Interview with April Koral, Writer's Digest, July, 1975, pp. 21-24.

The interview is concerned with White's experiences as a political reporter, as the author of two novels, as a researcher, and as an interviewer of political personages, especially Presidents, as well as his experiences with publishers. He says that he learned a great deal about writing from reading--he mentions particularly Herman Wouk, Henry Adams, and Edward Gibbon--and he thinks that reading and "getting edited" are important in helping the writer to learn techniques of structure and precision in the use of language.

WRITING ASSIGNMENTS

1. Read the various interviews by one of the following writers and write a paper in which you present the writer's views on writing: Ralph Ellison, William Faulkner, Robert Frost, Ernest Hemingway, Katherine Anne Porter, Robert Penn Warren, Eudora Welty.

2. Read the interviews in Lion in the Garden and write a paper in which you show the attitudes and ideas about writing expressed by Faulkner over the period covered by the interviews, 1926-1962.

3. Read the two versions of a sonnet written by Robert Frost in 1912 and 1936 and write a paper in which you discuss the changes that he made and the effect of the changes on the poem. Notice particularly the changes in the choice of words. The first version, "In White," is in The Dimensions of Robert Frost by Reginald L. Cook, 1958; the second version, "Design," is in Complete Poems of Robert Frost, 1964.

CHAPTER 2

WRITING AND LITERATURE

Reading in Relation to Writing
Writing in Various Literary Forms
Accounts of How Writing Was Done
Writing about Literature

"You [the student] will find a close relationship between learning to read well and learning to write well. A good reader is not necessarily a gifted writer, but he is nearly always an acceptable writer. What he has learned as a reader is the larger part of his equipment as a writer. Since language is a complex set of conventions, you cannot reasonably expect to use it well unless you know a good deal about the ways in which it has been used."

--Neal Frank Doubleday, Studies in Reading and Related Writing. Boston: D. C. Heath, 1957, p. 1.

"Reading is the work of the alert mind, is demanding, and under ideal conditions produces finally a sort of ecstasy. As in the sexual experience, there are never more than two persons present in the act of reading--the writer who is the impregnator, and the reader, who is the respondent. This gives the experience of reading a sublimity and power unequalled by any other form of communication."

--E. B. White, The Second Tree from the Corner. New York: Harper and Brothers, 1951, p. 161.

"It is not all books that are as dull as their readers.'

--Henry David Thoreau, Walden. Edited by J. Lyndon Shanley. Princeton University Press, 1971, p. 107.

"A list of books that you reread is like a clearing in the forest: a level, clean, well-lighted place where you set down your burdens and set up your home, your identity, your concerns, your continuity in a world that is at best indifferent, at worst malign."

--L. E. Sissman, "Innocent Bystander, The Constant Rereader's Five-Foot Shelf," The Atlantic, CCVIII (October, 1971), 34.

"To put it bluntly but realistically, a large number of our students never respond to literature because they never learn how to read it; I mean 'read it' in the ordinary sense of making out what it says."

--Seymour Chatman, "Reading Literature as Problem-Solving," English Journal, LII (1963), 346.

"One thing we can do is to read and write carefully, with as much precision as possible; for there are many thoughts that we cannot think without words, and to the extent that we think in words precision of language is the precision of thought."

--J. Mitchell Morse, "Are English Teachers Obsolete?" The CEA Critic, XXXVI (May, 1974), 11.

READING IN RELATION TO WRITING

Reading on the college level in any of the subject-
matter fields should be reading in "slow motion" and not
"speed-reading," for attention must be given not only to the
high points of interest, to thinking about what one has read,
but to transitions, to the special meanings of words in their
context, to the relation of sentence forms to meaning, and
to the levels of meaning above the exact meanings of the
words. Although reading may be a pure pleasure, unless
one "stands on tip-toe to read," as Thoreau suggests, he
may fail to strengthen his intellectual faculties. To read a
book as it should be calls for imagination, insight, and
judgment. One of the best ways to test one's understanding
of what he has read is to put his ideas into written form.

1. Anderson, Lee. "How Not to Read Poems--A
Dissenting View," in Art and the Craftsman, Best of the
Yale Literary Magazine, 1836-1961. Edited by Joseph Harnet
and Neil Goodwin. New Haven: Yale Literary Magazine,
1961, pp. 208-212.
Anderson thinks that the reason college graduates do
not read poetry after they leave college is that teachers of
poetry have emphasized examination of the text of poems and
neglected the pleasure principle which comes through oral
presentation. "It is wrong to see a poem before you hear
it." He says that in the teaching of poetry the most useful
function of oral interpretation is in determination of tone,
for it indicates the speaker's attitude toward his subject and
toward his audience. Anderson believes that if students have
the opportunity for listening room assignments, the audience
for poetry will increase and the number of students in writing
courses in poetry will also increase. Poets-to-be should use
the tape recorder in making their poems.

2. Brower, Reuben A. "Reading in Slow Motion,"

in In Defense of Reading. Edited by Reuben A. Brower and
Richard Poirier. New York: E. P. Dutton and Company,
Inc., 1962, pp. 3-21. Originally published in Reading for
Life: Developing the College Student's Lifetime Reading
Interest. Edited by Jacob M. Price. University of Michigan
Press, 1959.

    By "Reading in Slow Motion," Brower refers to the
"process of reading to observe what is happening, in order to
attend very closely to the words, their uses, and their meanings." He urges students to become "readers of the imagination." To illustrate his method of teaching students to become readers, Brower describes a course in slow reading
that he calls Literature X. In this course, he begins with
poems, then goes to a play by Shakespeare, to the reading of
a novel, to the relation of a work to its time, and thus into
history, and, as a final step, to a series of readings in such
writers as Chesterfield, Hume, and Dr. Johnson. All of
these writings have been approached through questions and
assignments that lead the student not only to read the work at
hand but to prepare him for reading the next work. At the
end of the first half of the course, the student is sent to read
and to interpret on his own another play by Sheakespeare and
another novel. He is given leading questions to direct him.
The mid-year examination may consist of a sight poem to interpret and an essay-exercise on a longer work outside of
class. The teaching of reading is necessarily the teaching of
writing. "The student cannot show his teacher or himself
that he has had an important and relevant literary experience
except in writing or in speaking that is as disciplined as good
writing."

    3. Chatman, Seymour. "Reading Literature as
Problem-Solving," English Journal, LII (1963), 346-352.
    Chatman says that students do not respond to literature
because they do not know how to read it, that is, they have
not developed the linguistic apparatus to read successfully.
He says that this apparatus contains three mechanisms: grammatical, lexical, and interpretational. The purpose of grammatical training in relation to reading is to teach the student
to make sense of sentences of various degrees of structural
complexity. Lexical analysis refers to the capacity to understand the proper sense of words in context. The interpretational problem requires the student to understand the probable
limits of reference in what he is reading. Chatman suggests
exercises and techniques to help students solve these three
problems.

4. Ciardi, John. "The Way to the Poem," in Dialogue with an Audience. Philadelphia: J. B. Lippincott, 1963, pp. 147-157.

A discussion of how Frost's "Stopping by Woods on a Snowy Evening" illustrates the way poetry works and how a poem means and how the poem should be read. Ciardi says that although the poem is a simple narration, it has a much larger meaning, a movement from the specific to the general. By a series of questions about the poem that he answers, Ciardi shows the structure, the purpose of the structure, and the meaning of the poem.

5. Gordon, Caroline. How to Read a Novel. New York: The Viking Press. Compass Books Edition, 1964. 248 pp. (Paper)

Caroline Gordon says that the best way to read a novel is to find out what the author attempts to do in the novel and to follow him as he does it. She illustrates her ideas by referring to specific works, beginning with Oedipus Rex, to illustrate complication and resolution, and continuing with Madame Bovary, to show the scene of a novel; War and Peace and Vanity Fair, to demonstrate a center of vision; to the first-person narrator in Farewell to Arms and in Faulkner; to the dramatic and central intelligence in Henry James; to tone, style, and controlling metaphor in Swift, Fielding, the Brontës, James, and Hawthorne; to the decline of the hero in Tom Jones; to Gertrude Stein and André Gide for formlessness. The last chapter concerns reading for enjoyment.

6. Nevins, Allan. "The Reading of History," in The Gateway to History. Boston: D. C. Heath and Company, 1938. Doubleday Anchor Book, Revised Edition, 1962, pp. 393-411.

History may be read for entertainment, for knowledge of the past, for guidance to the future, and for inspiration, but it does not offer easy entertainment and should be approached after careful preparation. The reading of nearly all history, says Nevins, requires application and should be the result of an aroused curiosity. Fortunately, current events as well as business and professional interests stimulate such curiosity. Business men want to read economic history; lawyers are interested in constitutional history; and literary people enjoy pure description and narration, memoirs and chronicles, travel accounts, historical novels and biographies. Quarrels about events cause people to read both sides of the issue. But a planned study with a view to breadth and depth is to be desired. Nevins thinks that the greatest lessons of history are moral and are closely related to the character of a nation. He suggests that the amateur reader read complete sets of books written by good historians to acquaint himself with large periods, but that such books be read in order of their "literary attractiveness."

7. Thoreau, Henry David. "Reading," in Walden. Edited by J. Lyndon Shanley. Princeton University Press, 1971, pp. 99-110.
Thoreau advocates the reading of the best books, for they are "the treasured wealth of the world and the fit inheritance of generations and nations." He thinks that the ancient classics should be read in the language in which they were written, and he believes that we should select only those writers for whom "we have to stand on tip-toe to read." He has no patience with those who waste their time with insignificant writers, for the "result is dullness of sight a stagnation of the vital circulations, and a general deliquium and sloughing off of all the intellectual faculties."

8. Woolf, Virginia, "How Should One Read a Book?" in The Second Common Reader. New York: Harcourt, Brace, and World, Inc., 1932, pp. 281-295.
Woolf says that a reader should not dictate to the author but should become his fellow-worker and accomplice. She suggests that perhaps the quickest way to understand what a novelist is doing is not to read, but to write. After an attempt to put an idea or impression into words, one can then turn to the opening pages of a good novel to see how a great writer handles a scene. Or we can read biographies and autobiographies to learn about people. Such reading helps to refresh and exercise our own creative powers. We can also read "rubbish-reading," not great writing but the records of ordinary people. Or we can turn to poetry for a more complete expression of truth. Then begins the process of comparing and thus the problem of judging and of forming our taste in reading. We begin to search for qualities common to entire books and to group them according to their common qualities. We may then turn to critics to help us to solidify our vague ideas, but they can help us only if we have profited from our own reading. To read a book as it should be calls for imagination, insight, and judgment.

WRITING ASSIGNMENTS

1. E. B. White says in "The Future of Reading," in The Second Tree from the Corner (New York: Harper and Brothers, 1951), p. 160, that doubt has been raised as to the future of reading, but that even if only one person should continue as a reader, he would be worth saving and should be the nucleus around which to found a university. He also suggests that the lone reader might well stand in the same relation to the community that a queen bee has to the colony of bees. The members of the community might dedicate themselves wholly to his welfare unless our modern hive of bees would try to perpetuate the race through audio-visual devices. Write a paper, humorous or otherwise, in which you depict such a situation.

WRITING IN VARIOUS LITERARY FORMS

The writing of poetry, drama, or fiction depends on the writer's ingenuity in acquiring ideas, on his knowledge of the form in which he writes, on his mastery of language, on his wide experience with literature through reading, on his willingness to work until his writing has attained a degree of excellence.

1. Abel, Lionel. "On Writing a Play," in On Creative Writing. Edited by Paul Engle. New York: E. P. Dutton and Company, Inc., Dutton Paperback, 1966, pp. 205-220.
Abel says that he can give only an abstract recipe for a play, for the writer of a play must find out for himself what it is needful for him to know. He thinks that all that happens in the plot of a play should, if possible, take place on the stage, keeping in mind the physical limits of the presentation and the cultural taste of the time. Abel discusses the qualities of a play--action, theme, characters, and dialogue--and illustrates his statements by referring to well-known plays. For him, dialogue is "the living element of the play, the medium in which the truth of the characters, the interest of the action, the importance of the theme, the ability of the character or characters to join theme to action are determined."

2. Galsworthy, John. "Some Platitudes Concerning Drama," in A Preface to College Prose. Edited by Charles Gott and John A. Behnke. New York: Macmillan Company, 1936, pp. 353-360. Originally published in Inn of Tranquillity, Charles Scribner's Sons, 1912.
Galsworthy says that a drama must be shaped to have meaning and that the shaping of life and character has its inherent moral. It is thus the business of the dramatist to pose the group so as to show the moral. He thinks that

there are three courses open to the serious dramatist: to
set before the public the views and codes of life it believes
in; to set before the public the views and codes of life which
the dramatist believes in and lives; to set before the public
the phenomena of life and character, selected and combined
by the dramatist's outlook, with the public left to draw the
moral. He discusses the main qualities of drama: plot,
action, character, dialogue, and flavor, the last of which
he says is the essential attribute of any art.

3. Justice, Donald. "On the Writing of Poetry," in
On Creative Writing. Edited by Paul Engle. New York:
E. P. Dutton and Company, Inc. Dutton Paperback Edition,
1966, pp. 127-142.
Justice lists three propositions that have to do with
the special character of poetry and discusses each in detail.
These propositions are: the form of a poem is more directly apprehensible than the ordinary larger and looser
forms of the novel or play; the words of a poem are different from the words of a novel in that they demand more
attention in their own right; the rhythm of a poem, since it
binds and sustains other elements, is itself an object of
interest. He adds a fourth characteristic of poetry, the
making of images, but says that this is also a characteristic
of the novel, the story, and the play. He says that the poet
gains his understanding of the character of poetry by writing
poems, but his understanding is partly intuitive and will constantly change.

4. Spender, Stephen. "The Making of a Poem," in
The Making of a Poem. New York: W. W. Norton and
Company, Inc., Norton Library Edition, 1962, pp. 45-62.
Spender says that the writer of poetry should be able
to think in images and to have a mastery of language. He
emphasizes the importance of concentration, inspiration,
memory, faith in the vocation, and song as elements of
making a poem. He says that he dreads writing poetry, for
the writing brings one face to face with his own personality.
He illustrates his method for obtaining ideas for poetry by
referring to his use of a notebook which he has kept for
several years.

5. Welty, Eudora. "The Reading and Writing of
Short Stories," The Atlantic Monthly, CLXXXII (February,
1959), 54-58; (March, 1949), 46-49.
Welty says that the writing of a story is creation in
imagination, and that the analysis of a story tears it down to

its elements. She thinks that criticism or analysis is an impossible way to learn how a story was written, for one cannot thus go back to the starting point of inspiration. The reading of a story should be enjoyable; it should read new and should not be the result of "instructor, advised readers, victims of summaries and textbooks." But she says that she does not mean that we should be easy on the story, but not to interpret it as if the "conscience were at stake." Welty illustrates her comments on story writing and analysis by referring to stories by Hemingway, Faulkner, Forster, Lawrence, Crane, and Mansfield.

6. Wilder, Thornton. "Some Thoughts on Play-writing," in Aspects of the Drama, a Handbook, by Sylvan Barnet, Morton Berman, and William Burto. Boston: Little, Brown and Company, 1962, pp. 1-11.

Wilder presents and explains four fundamental conditions of drama which he says separate it from the other arts: it depends on the work of many collaborators; it is addressed to the group mind; it is based upon a pretense; its action takes place in the present.

7. "The Writing of Poetry," in Teaching Creative Writing. Washington, D.C.: Library of Congress, 1974, pp. 26-64.

The Conference on Teaching Creative Writing, January 29-30, 1973, at the Library of Congress, had as members of the panel for the writing of poetry the following writers: Paul Engle, chairman; Michael Dennis Browne, John Ciardi, Elliott Coleman, Josephine Jacobsen, Anthony McNeill, N. Scott Momaday, and Miller Williams. Engle points out some of the advantages and the risks of having creative writing courses in college. He believes that not only the language of poetry can be taught, but the vision as well. He says that although intuition may be the origin of a poem, working it out on the page is the result of the whole man and requires work. Other members of the panel mention the fact that young poets have not read much poetry. They also stress the idea that teachers of poetry writing should demand a standard of excellence from their students.

WRITING ASSIGNMENTS

1. Locate and read at least three additional articles on the writing of a play, a story, a novel, or a poem, and write a paper in which you present the ideas about writing found in the article.

ACCOUNTS OF HOW WRITING WAS DONE

Why writers write, where they get ideas and materials for writing, how and when they write, how they solve the problems they incur in writing, and to whom they turn when they need assistance--these are some of the questions answered in the articles and books included in this section. Although it is sometimes difficult for a writer to pinpoint the source of his material, many of the writers included in this section use their own experiences and observations, memories of their childhood, written accounts, historical data, interviews and stories, as the basis of their writing, but all of them emphasize the idea that imagination must act on the raw data to produce an artistic product. The writers indicate that they have problems in finding the proper form in which to present their material, in creating believable characters, and in using language suited to purpose and characters. Several mention the value of editorial assistance. Irving Wallace says (The Writing of One Novel, pp. 21-22) that he had learned "less about writing and received less encouragement from English instructors than I have from reading and listening to a working artist relate how a single creation--poem, play, short story, novel--was brought to life and to maturity and to its public place."

1. Afterwords, Novelists on Their Novels. Edited by Thomas McCormack. New York: Harper and Row, 1969. 229 pp.
Accounts by fourteen modern writers on how they wrote particular novels.

2. Bradbury, Ray. "Commentary: Seeds of Three Stories," in On Writing by Writers. Edited by William M. West. Boston: Ginn and Co., 1966, pp. 48-59.
Bradbury tells how he came to write "There Will Come Soft Rains," "Forever and the Earth," and "I See You

Never." The inspiration for the first story came from a poem by the same name by Sara Teasdale. The second story came from the desire to prolong the life of Thomas Wolfe, who had died at an early age. The third is based on an actual experience Bradbury had while living in a mixed-racial area of Los Angeles.

3. Buck, Pearl S. "The Writing of East Wind: West Wind," in Breaking into Print. Edited by Elmer Adler. New York: Simon and Schuster, 1937, pp. 29-34. Originally appeared in Part Twelve of The Colophon, December, 1932.
Written on an English steamship while Pearl Buck was crossing the Pacific, East Wind: West Wind first appeared in Asia Magazine under the title of A Chinese Woman Speaks. A few years later, another story was added as a sequel; it was published by the John Day Company after Pearl Buck had deleted trite phrases, the use of which was considered good literary style in China.

4. Canfield, Dorothy. "How 'Flint and Fire' Started and Grew," in Americans All. Edited by Benjamin A. Heydrick, 1920. Reprinted by Books for Libraries Press, 1971, pp. 210-223.
Dorothy Canfield says that for her the beginning of a story is in a greater than usual sensitiveness to emotion. It may be any emotion, but she recognizes it as the right one when it brings with it an impulse to make other people feel it. "Flint and Fire" had its beginning in a chance encounter with an old man who had a tragic element in his life. In the midst of her common household duties, she continued to work out the elements of the plot and to decide on how the story would be told. The story was then written at white heat. Sometimes she wrote for four hours at a time, with rewriting, compression, and technical revision every morning. Part of it was read aloud to catch clumsy phrasing. It was also read for suggestiveness, for correction of facts, and revision for movement, for sound, sense proportion, and grammar.

5. Cather, Willa. "On Death Comes for the Archbishop," in Willa Cather on Writing. Critical Studies in Writing as an Art. With a Foreword by Stephen Tennant. New York: Alfred A. Knopf, 1959, pp. 3-13.
Cather tells how she became interested in the work of the Catholic priests and in the beauty of the old mission churches when she first went into the Southwest. She became

acquainted with Father Haltermann, a Belgian priest, who
served eighteen Indian missions in New Mexico, and she
heard many stories of the work of Archbishop Lamy, the
first bishop of New Mexico. In Santa Fe, she found a book
printed several years before on a country press in Pueblo,
Colorado. This was The Life of the Right Reverend Joseph
P. Machebeuf by William Joseph Howlett, a priest who
worked with Father Machebeuf in Denver. This book revealed as much about Father Lamy as about Father Machebeuf and contained letters of Father Machebeuf to his sister
in France giving details of his life in New Mexico. Cather
says that she had wanted to write something in the style of
legend, in which mood and not situation is the main thing.
The mood and spirit she found in Father Machebeuf's letters,
but in order to convey the "hardihood of the spirit," she
says that she had to make the language a little stiff and to
use the trite phraseology of the frontier. She says that she
followed the life story of the two bishops much as it was,
but included many of her own experiences as well as some
of her father's. The actual writing took only a few months.

      6.   Cheever, John. "What Happened," in Under-
standing Fiction. Edited by Cleanth Brooks and Robert Penn
Warren. Second Edition. New York: Appleton-Century-
Crofts, Inc., 1959, pp. 570-572.
      Cheever's account of how he wrote "Goodbye, My
Brother." It is based partly on his own experience in
spending a long summer on Martha's Vineyard, combined
with other experiences of his own and those of his family
and friends, and his feelings after returning to his home in
Manhattan.

      7.   Cosbey, Robert C. "Thoreau at Work: The
Writing of 'Ktaadn,'" in The Writer's Job by Robert C.
Cosbey. Atlanta: Scott, Foresman and Company, 1966,
pp. 247-257. Reprinted from the Bulletin of the New York
Public Library, LXV, No. 1, January, 1961.
      Cosbey gives an account, based on an unpublished
journal in the Berg Collection of the New York Public Library, of how Thoreau wrote "Ktaadn." Thoreau kept notes
of his experience and observations while making an excursion
into the Maine wilderness in September, 1846. After
Thoreau returned to his cabin at Walden Pond, he began to
expand his notes in his notebook. This was followed by a
first draft which includes expansions of certain parts of the
trip but with little attention to order and time. There were
many corrections--deletions, insertions, substitutions,

additions--but at that time he had not yet found a unifying
theme. Between the first draft and the published version
(Cosbey suggests there may have been other drafts which
we do not have), Thoreau had arrived at the idea of wilderness as the theme. The first published version is "the
achievement of a simple, unified narrative and a fitting,
consistent tone." Even after the essay was published in
1848, Thoreau continued to make changes and the final
version which appeared in The Maine Woods, 1864, contained changes in style, corrections of typographical errors,
and additional information about the Maine woods based on
his reading. There were also changes that involved Thoreau's ideas about Indians.

     8. Durham, Frank. "Porgy: Work in Progress,"
in DuBose Heyward, the Man Who Wrote Porgy. Columbia:
University of South Carolina Press, 1954. Reissued by the
Kennikat Press, Inc., 1965, pp. 49-62.
     Frank Durham bases his account of how DuBose Hey-
ward wrote Porgy on versions of the novel now at the
Charleston Library Society. He discusses the development
of the character of Porgy, the representation of Catfish Row,
the construction of the plot, the relationship between the
Negroes of Catfish Row and the white characters, the use
of Negro spirituals and of Gullah speech.

     9. Eliot, George. "Scenes of Clerical Life," and
"History of 'Adam Bede,'" in The Letters of George Eliot.
Selected with an Introduction by R. Brimley Johnson. London:
Macveagh. New York: The Dial Press, 1927, pp. 198-214.
     In letters to John Blackwood, June 11 and August 17,
1857, George Eliot explains the "spirit and future course" of
"Scenes of Clerical Life" and tells her publisher that she,
as an artist, cannot make changes in the language or character but is willing to change mere details. She says that
some of her material is based on fact, but some of the
details have been filled in from her imagination. In "History
of 'Adam Bede,'" taken from her Journal, Eliot says that the
germ of the novel was an anecdote told her by her aunt in
1839 or 1840 and the character of Adam was suggested by
her father's early life. She began to write the novel on
October 22, 1857. The book was published a year later by
Blackwood. She was paid 800 pounds for four years' copyright.

     10. Farrell, James T. "How Studs Lonigan Was
Written," in The Theory of the American Novel. Edited with

an Introduction by George Perkins. New York: Holt, Rinehart and Winston, 1970, pp. 403-410. Included as the introduction to the Modern Library Studs Lonigan, New York,
1938.
     Farrell says that he began writing what developed into
the trilogy in June, 1929. In the spring of 1929, he took a
course in advanced composition conducted by Professor James
Weber Linn at the University of Chicago. One of the stories
he wrote for this class was entitled Studs. After Professor
Linn had read the story to the class and had praised it en-
thusiastically, Farrell asked Professor Robert Morse Lovett
to read it. Lovett suggested that the story be developed at
greater length. As Farrell continued to work on the material, the book expanded and finally grew into three novels.
Farrell says that he thought of Studs Lonigan as the story
of an American destiny in our time since it deals with the
making and the education of an ordinary American boy.

     11. Gallico, Paul. "The Snow Goose: The Back-
ground," in Confessions of a Story Writer. New York:
Alfred A. Knopf, 1946, pp. 490-494.
     Gallico says that his imagination was stimulated by
the story of the evacuation at Dunkirk to write a story of
the courage and bravery of these men. While living in a
rented apartment in San Francisco, he had read Kipling's
stories. He says that at this time there were three ingredients loose in his head that fitted into his tale: Dunkirk;
a painter, Peter Scott; and the British tommies of Soldiers
Three. From Scott he borrowed his art, his lighthouse,
and his bird-sanctuary. Gallico says that he wrote half a
dozen pages but threw them away and began all over with
the idea of the snow goose to pull the story together. He
made Philip Rhayader a hunchback to explain why he was
not in the war. The story was rejected by The Saturday
Evening Post until he rewrote the ending.

     12. Baum, Catherine B., and Floyd C. Watkins.
"Caroline Gordon and 'The Captive': An Interview," Southern
Review, VII, ii (1971), 447-462.
     In the winter of 1966, while Caroline Gordon was
teaching creative writing at Emory University, Catherine B.
Baum and Floyd C. Watkins interviewed Miss Gordon on how
she wrote the story, "The Captive," based on an account of
captivity by the Indians of Mrs. Jennie Wiley and told by
William Esley Connelly in The Founding of Harman's Station
with an Account of the Indian Captivity of Mrs. Jennie Wiley
and the Exploration and Settlement of the Big Sandy Valley in

the Virginias and Kentucky, New York, 1910. The questions
concern changes and additions that Gordon made in the account, her use of folk songs and tales and her use of dialect,
her attitudes toward themes and symbols, and her use of
the supernatural.

13. Mann, Thomas. The Story of a Novel. The
Genesis of Doctor Faustus. Translated from the German
by Richard and Clara Winston. New York: Alfred A.
Knopf, 1961. 233 pp. Excerpt included in The Writer's
Craft, edited by John Hersey. New York: Alfred A. Knopf,
1974, pp. 362-373.
Mann's account, chapter by chapter, of the writing of
Dr. Faustus, as well as an account of the origin and develop-
ment of the novel.

14. O'Neill, Eugene. "Working Notes and Extracts
from a Fragmentary Work Diary," in American Playwrights
on Drama. Edited by Horst Frenz. New York: Hill and
Wang. Dramabook, 1965, pp. 3-15.
Notes covering the period from Spring, 1926 to September, 1931 give O'Neill's own account of how he wrote
Mourning Becomes Electra.

15. Owens, William A. "Writing a Novel--Problem
and Solution," Southwest Review, XL (Summer, 1955), 254-
261.
An account of how Owens became interested in writing
and of how he wrote Walking on Borrowed Land. Owens
tells how he chose and created the characters and how he
did the actual writing. He discusses the choice of language
and the selection of scenes, from memory and by creation.
He concludes that it is impossible to tell exactly how the
novel was written; he can only point out some of the devices.
He believes that writing "comes right" when the writer is
willing to submerge himself in his characters and in their
way of life.

16. Porter, Katherine Anne. "Noon Wine: The
Sources," in The Art of Writing Fiction. By Ray B. West,
Jr. New York: Thomas Y. Crowell Company, 1968, pp.
67-80. Originally appeared in the Yale Review, Autumn,
1956.
Porter explains that her story is fiction but that many
of the characters and incidents are made up of things that
actually happened; the events are changed and reshaped and
interpreted. She thinks that her story is "true" in the way

a work of fiction should be true, "created out of all the
scattered particles of life I was able to absorb and combine
and to shape into a living new being."

17. Rawlings, Marjorie Kinnan. Letter to Maxwell
Perkins on the background of South Moon Under, in The
Marjorie Kinnan Rawlings Reader. Selected and edited with
an Introduction by Julia Scribner Bingham. New York:
Charles Scribner's Sons, 1956, pp. xi-xiii.
    In the fall of 1931, Mrs. Rawlings went to live for
several weeks deep in the scrub country of Florida, with
an old woman and her moonshiner son, to gather material
for a novel. Later, she wrote a letter to her editor,
Maxwell Perkins, about the people, their lives, their language, and how she planned to use these in what became
South Moon Under, a novel published in 1933.

18. Rosten, Leo. "Preface. The Confessions of
Mr. Parkhill," in The Return of H*Y*M*A*N K*A*P*L*A*N.
New York: Harper and Brothers, 1938, 1959, pp. 9-20.
    Rosten explains how he came to write the stories of
Mr. Kaplan and asks and answers some questions about himself, the characters, and the writing of his books. He says
that comic dialect is very tricky to write, for it "must seduce
the eye to reach the ear and be orchestrated in the brain.
It must tantalize without irritating, and defer without frus-
trating." The problem of dialect is complicated when the
characters write as well as speak. Rosten says that he
writes because of the need to communicate and to be understood. Writing, he says, is an internal dialogue in which
one part of himself tries to make itself understood by another. A writer's deepest satisfaction is in the writing itself.

19. Steinbeck, John. Journal of a Novel. The East
of Eden Letters. New York: The Viking Press, 1969.
Bantam Edition, 1970. 242 pp.
    In writing East of Eden, Steinbeck prepared himself
for writing each day by writing a letter to his editor, Pascal
Covici. The letters appeared on the left-hand pages of his
notebook; on the right he wrote the text of the novel. The
writing covered the period from January 29 through November
1, 1951, with a letter for each working day until the first
draft of the novel was finished. The letters are concerned
with thoughts about the novel, about novel-writing in general,
with ideas of the creative process, as well as about Steinbeck
himself.

20. Wallace, Irving. The Writing of One Novel.
New York: Simon and Schuster, 1969. 250 pp.
An account of how Wallace gained the idea for writing
The Prize, a novel based on the Nobel Prize awards, and
of how he collected information and worked on it at intervals
from 1946 to June 11, 1962, when the novel was published.
The book is divided into four parts: Conception, Gestation,
Birth, and Appendix, which includes "Work Chart of a Novel,"
and a "Synopsis of The Prize." In the "Work Chart," Wallace
summarizes the work of the novel by sections and concludes
that he spent 582 days and 3,101 man hours working on the
novel.

21. Warren, Robert Penn. "Andrew Lytle's The
Long Night," in Rediscoveries. Edited and with an Introduction by David Madden. New York: Crown Publishers, Inc.,
1971, pp. 17-28. Originally published in the Southern Review.
Warren tells how in the 1930's, the historian Frank
Owsley told him a tale which had been told to him by his
great-uncle, a tale that went back to the 1850's, of how
Owsley's great-grandfather was shot to death in his bed by
a gang of men who had burst into his house, while his wife
and young son looked on. The young boy became obsessed
with vengeance and spent his life tracking down and killing
all but two or three of the murderers. These he wanted
Frank to track down and kill. Dr. Owsley told the same
tale to Andrew Lytle, who used it as the basis of The Long
Night, a novel published in 1936. Warren explains what
Lytle did to the story to turn the tale into an artistic production. He gives it a world, a form which shows the relations between scene and action and character. The main
change is in the nature of the avenger, who once he is
started in his vengeance becomes only his "role," but for
the novelist this is not enough and he adds the Civil War to
constitute a deeper drama. But the "great public bloodletting"
drains the avenger of his private thirst for blood, and he decides to desert and to go far away from the world and vengeance.

22. Warren, Robert Penn. "How a Story Was Born
and How, Bit by Bit, It Grew," in Opinions and Perspectives
from The New York Times Book Review. Edited by Francis
Brown. Baltimore: Penguin Books, Inc., 1966, pp. 307-313.
Included in Brooks and Warren, Understanding Fiction, Second
Edition, 1959, pp. 638-643, in a different version.

An account of how Warren wrote the story, "Black-
berry Winter," in the winter of 1945-1946, just after the
war when he had been reading Melville's poetry, especially
a poem about the Civil War. Warren had just finished
writing All the King's Men and making a study of "The Ancient
Mariner." He was living in a "blizzard hit Northern city"
and he began to think of his boyhood in the South and of his
being allowed to go barefoot in early spring and of a cold
spell. Warren insists that the story is not autobiographical.

23. Warren, Robert Penn. "The Way It Was Written," The New York Times Book Review, August 23, 1953,
pp. 6, 25.
An account of the writing of "Brother to Dragons."
Warren says that he had been interested in doing something
with the story of Thomas Jefferson's family in Kentucky for
about ten years. He first thought of using the material in
a novel but abandoned the idea as he did that of using it as
a play. He decided on the form of a dramatic dialogue
since this form would allow him more freedom in presenting
the issues and in widening the perspective. He says that he
developed the character of Lucy and introduced Meriwether
Lewis to redeem Jefferson from "mere shock and mere
repudiation of his old dream." He encountered three particular problems in the poem: keeping the episodes sharp
in both symbolic and narrative sense, using language suitable to the various characters, and "keeping interest and
readability at the level of action and debate and at the same
time keeping that inwardness that is the central fact of
poetry."

24. Wharton, Edith. "Introduction," Ethan Frome.
New York: Charles Scribner's Sons, 1911, pp. v-x.
In this introduction, Wharton explains the construction
of Ethan Frome and the problems involved in using the form
chosen. One problem was how to deal with a subject of
which the dramatic climax occurs a generation later than
the first acts of the tragedy. Another problem was to find
ways of bringing the tragedy to the knowledge of the narrator
because of the "deeprooted reticence and inarticulateness of
the people," and to achieve the effect of "roundness" produced by letting the situation be told by two characters who
tell only what each is capable of understanding. The narrator sees it all and resolves the situation.

25. Wharton, Edith. "The Writing of Ethan Frome,"
in Breaking into Print. Edited by Elmer Adler. New York:

Simon and Schuster, 1937, pp. 189-191.
Edith Wharton says that she began Ethan Frome in
French as an exercise for perfecting her knowledge of the
language. But this was abandoned and a few years later
she wrote the novel in English. She refutes the idea that
Henry James suggested the story and the idea that she was
unfamiliar with the New England scene, for she had spent
about ten years in the New England hill country and knew its
people--their dialect as well as their attitudes and hardships.

26. Wolfe, Thomas. The Story of a Novel. New
York: Charles Scribner's Sons, 1936, 1964.
An account of the writing of Of Time and the River
with the editorial assistance of Maxwell Perkins, who tells
him when the novel is finished since Wolfe had the urge to
tell all he knew and seemed unable to stop writing.

WRITING ASSIGNMENTS

1. Robert Penn Warren says in "The Way It Was
Written" that he thought of using the Jefferson material in
a novel and as a play but abandoned both forms for the form
of a dramatic dialogue. Read "Brother to Dragons" and
write a paper in which you discuss the advantages in the
form he chose and show why the material is not suited for
the form of a novel or of a play.

2. Write a paper in which you compare the completed work with the original story or character that served
as a basis for the writing, and arrive at some conclusions
about why an accurate portrayal of an actual person cannot
be used in imaginative writing. The Fabulous Originals by
Irving Wallace (New York: Alfred A. Knopf, 1956) includes
accounts of several living persons who were used by writers
as originals of their characters: Sherlock Holmes, Dr.
Jekyll and Mr. Hyde, Marie Roget, Robinson Crusoe, etc.

3. In the preface to An Autobiographical Novel
(Garden City, N.Y.: Doubleday and Company, Inc., 1966),
Kenneth Rexroth says that he "did not actually write the book
but talked it." He began by talking into a tape recorder.
He then revised the tapes by redictating them. Read portions, or all of the book, point out examples in which oral
style differs from written style, and draw conclusions as
to the effectiveness of "talking" instead of "writing" for good
writing.

4. Read Willie Morris's North Toward Home (Boston: Houghton Mifflin Company, 1967) and "Down Home," John Carr's interview with Willie Morris in Kite-Flying and Other Irrational Acts, pp. 96-119, and write a paper organized into two sections. In the first section discuss the material that Morris uses as the basis of his book and in the second section discuss what you have learned about writing from Morris's accounts. He says that he began the book as fiction and finished it as autobiography. Where does a writer get his material? What is Morris's attitude toward his material? Describe his style of writing. List any experiences of your own that you recalled from reading this book that you may use as the basis of your own writing.

5. Read Hervey Allen's novel, Anthony Adverse, and his account of where he obtained the material for the novel in "The Sources of 'Anthony Adverse,'" The Saturday Review of Literature, X (January 13, 1934), 401; 408-410, and write a paper in which you relate his account to the finished novel.

6. Read Willa Cather's account of how she wrote Death Comes for the Archbishop and Edward A. Bloom and Lillian D. Bloom, "The Genesis of Death Comes for the Archbishop," American Literature, XXVI (January, 1955), 480-506, and write a paper in which you combine and compare the two accounts.

7. In Stephen Crane, a Biography, 1968, pp. 237-260, Robert W. Stallman gives an account of the Commodore disaster, the wreck of the ship off the coast of Florida that Crane uses as the basis of his story "The Open Boat," and compares Crane's story with the original account. Read the story and Stallman's account and write a paper on how Crane used a factual account as the basis of literary art. Point out particularly Crane's use of imagery and metaphorical language. You may want to read also Richard P. Adams, "Naturalistic Fiction: 'The Open Boat,'" Tulane Studies in English, IX (1954), 137-146.

WRITING ABOUT LITERATURE

There are many books and articles designed to provide students with ideas and ways of writing about literature,
but the approaches to a piece of writing and the methods of
analysis are about as numerous as the individuals who write
and the writing that is being analyzed. The items to be considered depend on the type of writing, the period to which it
belongs, and its relation to similar pieces of writing and to
its place in the author's development as a writer. There
seems to be no limit to the subjects that may interest a
writer: sources, ideas, structure, language, style, etc.
A simple outline to keep in mind is to try to answer three
questions about a piece of writing: What is the author's
purpose? How does he do it? Was it worth doing? These
simplified are purpose, material, method, evaluation. For
beginning students, the last may be omitted since proper
evaluation depends on wide knowledge and experience in
reading.

For this section, only a few examples of critical essays have been included: a study of backgrounds, rhetorical
movements, character, imagery, appreciation, analysis of a
poem.

1. Clemen, Wolfgang. "Hamlet, " in The Development of Shakespeare's Imagery. Cambridge, Mass.: Harvard
University Press, 1951, pp. 106-118.
Clemen discusses the relation of Hamlet's imagery to
the atmosphere and theme of the play, to his wide educational
background and experience, to his changing moods, to his
ability to penetrate to the real nature of man, to his feigned
madness, to the foreshadowing of the final catastrophe, and
to the tone of the play.

2. Conrad, Joseph. "Henry James: An Appreciation, " in Notes on Life and Letters. Memorial Edition, XIX.

With an Introduction by William Rothenstein. Garden City, N.Y.: Doubleday, Page and Co., 1925, pp. 11-19.

In this essay, written two years before the appearance of the New York Edition of James's work, Conrad laments the lack of a collected edition of James. He says that after twenty years of reading James, he is grateful for the sense of happiness James has brought. He compares the volume and force of his work to those of a majestic river. Conrad says that it will be the artist, the imaginative man, who will be the last speaker "on the eve of that day without tomorrow." One of these choice souls is Henry James, "the historian of fine conscience," for he has mastered "the country, his domain, not wild indeed, but full of romantic glimpses of deep shadows and sunny places."

3. Ellmann, Richard. "The Backgrounds of 'The Dead,'" in James Joyce. New York: Oxford University Press, 1959, pp. 252-263.

Ellmann says that although the story of "The Dead" deals mainly with three generations of Joyce's family in Dublin, it also draws upon an incident in Galway in 1903. In Galway, Nora Barnacle (later Mrs. James Joyce) was courted by Michael Bodkin, who was confined to bed because of tuberculosis. When Nora decided to go to Dublin, Bodkin stole out of his sickroom, in spite of rainy weather, to sing to her and bid her goodbye. Soon he was dead. Ellmann also mentions one of Thomas Moore's Irish Melodies called "O, Ye Dead!" that Joyce learned to sing. Joyce begins "The Dead" with a party and ends with a corpse, and thus introduces Irish traditions. Ellmann quotes Stanislaus Joyce as saying that the speech of Gabriel Conroy is a good imitation of his father's oratorical style. Many of the party guests come from Joyce's recollections. Joyce also attributes some of his own experiences to Gabriel. The letter which Gabriel remembers having written to Gretta Conroy contains sentences from a letter that Joyce wrote to Nora in 1904. Joyce also wrote book reviews as does Gabriel Conroy. The physical image of Gabriel with his hair parted in the middle and wearing rimmed glasses also came from Joyce. Ellmann says that Joyce borrowed the ending for the story from George Moore's Vain Fortune.

4. Epstein, E. L. "Hopkins's 'Heaven-Haven': A Linguistic-Critical Description," Essays in Criticism, XXIII (April, 1973), 137-145.

Epstein uses Hopkins's "Heaven-Haven" to show how a literary critic may use linguistic analysis to arrive at the

meaning of a poem. He discusses five points at which tex-
tural details reinforce the meaning: use of vagueness to express time; other "detemporalizing" devices such as word
choice, tense, meaning versus syntax; use of conjunction and
to neutralize temporal progression; syntactic structure to
reinforce the subjective sense of the poem; use of the partial
hendiadys of "sharp and sifed" to add to the subjective im-
port of the poem.

5. Heilman, Robert B. "Ship of Fools, Notes on
Style," in Katherine Anne Porter: A Critical Symposium.
Edited by Lodwick Hartley and George Core. Athens, Ga.:
University of Georgia Press, 1969, pp. 197-210.
Heilman says that the style of Ship of Fools is not
imposed from without but is rather an emanation of the materials themselves. Porter's style, he says, is a fusion of
proved styles. She can do ordinary documentary; she can
combine words unexpectedly without being ostentatious; she
uses strong metaphors; she has a talent for summarizing
sequence; she has a comic sense that is suffused with irony;
she has an eye for precision as shown in her language and
syntax. Heilman thinks that Porter's style has strong affilia-
tions with the styles of Jane Austen and George Eliot and
thus its main lines are traditional.

6. Knox, Bernard. "Sophocles' Oedipus," in Tragic
Themes in Western Literature. Edited with an Introduction
by Cleanth Brooks. New Haven: Yale University Press,
1955, pp. 7-29.
Knox traces the character and actions of Oedipus
throughout the plays from his position of "the first of men"
to his terrible reversal at the close of Oedipus the King.
Since the reward of Oedipus, whose main flaw is only his
desire to know, seems unjust, Sophocles wrote Oedipus at
Colonus in which Oedipus is rewarded by being "equated with
the gods" at his death. Knox says that Oedipus is not only
the greatest creation of a major poet, he is also a symbol
of human aspiration and despair.

7. Ross, Francis D. "Rhetorical Procedure in
Thoreau's 'Battle of the Ants,'" College Composition and
Communication, XVI (February, 1965), 14-18.
Ross sees four movements in Thoreau's battle of the
ants: the author's literal description of the fighting ants
written from the viewpoint of an omniscient observer; the
shift in the point of view of the narrator from literal action
to allegory when the ants become mythical heroes fighting the

Trojan War; the narrator becomes a part of the Revolutionary War and of the Concord battle; the narrator views the ant fighters as human fighters and the ant war as a human one. Ross says the shifts in perspective give the reader both literal and allegorical views of the conflict. The close-up perspective of the narrator behind the magnifying glass is "the trick of the first-person narrative form in the hands of the artist-poet that leads us to understand and record his insights throughout the passage."

     8.   Tate, Allen. "Because I Could Not Stop for Death," (#712, The Chariot), in The Man of Letters in the Modern World, Selected Essays: 1928-1955. New York: Meridian Books, 1955, pp. 218-221.
     Tate says that this poem of Emily Dickinson is one of the greatest in the English language, for it is "flawless to the last detail." He bases his judgment on the relation of rhythm to the pattern of the poem, the precise images which fuse with the central idea, the presentation of the theme of death without offering a solution. The framework, the abstractions of mortality and eternity, associate perfectly with the images. "No poet could have invented the elements of The Chariot; only a great poet could have used them so perfectly." Tate comments on Dickinson's precision of statement and her diction, which he says consists of words of Latin and Greek origin used against words of concrete Saxon element.

WRITING ASSIGNMENTS

     1.   Read several critical articles on poetry, stories, novels, dramas, or non-fiction prose and from these articles prepare an outline to be used in examining one of these types of writing.

     2.   Select a topic based on a piece of writing that you are studying at the present time and write a paper concerned with some aspect of the writing or with the writing as a whole.

     3.   Read Frost's comments on writing poetry that he gives in letters, prefaces, reviews, interviews, and lectures, and write a paper presenting his ideas. You will find his comments in Robert Frost on Writing, edited by Elaine Barry, Rutgers University Press, 1973.

4. Read Charles Morgan's novel, <u>Sparkenbroke</u>, Macmillan, 1936, and write a paper in which you bring together Morgan's ideas about writing as they are expressed in the statements and actions of Lord Sparkenbroke.

CHAPTER 3

WRITING IN
HISTORY
BIOGRAPHY & AUTOBIOGRAPHY
LAW

"No form of literature is nobler, more instructive or more moving than a history of great events greatly related. History sometimes stumbles, but it offers the only sure key we shall ever find to the complex world, the surest guide to judgment and the soundest set of standards."

--Allan Nevins, "The Telling of a Nation's Story," in Opinions and Perspectives from The New York Times Book Review. Edited by Francis Brown. Baltimore: Penguin Books, Inc., 1966, p. 378.

"A people without history
Is not redeemed from time, for history is a pattern
Of timeless moments."

--T. S. Eliot, "Little Gidding," from Four Quartets

"Every human being needs direct personal contact with the great stories, myths, and fictions of the human race, and with history, to begin to know himself and to sense the potentialities--of all sorts, for good and for bad-- that lie within his reach and the reach of other men. The reaches of the human soul and the distortions the human mind is capable of, the meanness that often mars our judg- ments and the great liberations we can achieve, what it is to be a man and what it can be, these things are known through the lives and actions of individuals who speak to us by means of art and the pages of history."

--Nathan M. Pusey, "The Centrality of Humanistic Study," in The Humanities, An Appraisal. Edited by Julian Harris. University of Wisconsin Press, 1962, p. 80.

THE WRITING OF HISTORY

The writer of history encounters the same problems that writers of other subjects encounter--selecting and limiting the subject, locating adequate data, organizing and writing in clear and logical prose. In addition, he must be intellectually honest and confine himself to facts, and he cannot invent except to weave facts into an intelligible pattern. The dilemma of historians as to whether history is a science based on objective data, or is an art, a form of literature, seems to have been decided by modern historians in favor of history as an art, for history must be read if it is to affect society and it must be interesting if it is read. The modern historian has a variety of material at his disposal which was not available to historians of the past, but he must be more exacting in his standards and he must choose his material with greater care. But he has a wider field than political history, the accounts of battles, and the exploits of heroes, for he must tell the story of the bottom levels of society as well as of those at the top, of man's failures as well as of his successes, and "even the subliminal elements of life in the past." Nothing is too insignificant for his use as long as he relates it to the total picture of man's activities and confines himself to what is known.

1. Adams, James Truslow. "My Methods as a Historian," in Writing for Love or Money. Edited by Norman Cousins. New York: Longmans, Green, and Company, 1949, pp. 176-185.
Adams says that history is not a science since history is personal and science is impersonal. He believes that the philosophy of history is a combination of the great man theory and the influence of social forces. He thinks that the qualities of mind required to write sound history are more akin to those of the artist than to those of the scientist, but

this does not mean that history should be written as fiction. "The historian must stick to his facts as he finds them, but in finding them and in weaving them together he needs not only the scientist's love of truth but delicate intuition, experience of men and affairs, and other qualities a scientist does not need in his work."

2. Bean, Walton. "Is Clio a Muse?" Sewanee Review, XLV (1937), 419-426.
Bean welcomes the broadening of the scope of history to include the whole economic, social, and cultural part of man. He says that it is difficult to distinguish between academic social history and popular art--literature, the dance, painting, etc.--and since Clio is a Muse, there should not be quarreling between historians and artists.

3. Beard, Charles A. "Written History as an Act of Faith," American Historical Review, XXXIX (January, 1934), 219-229.
Beard attacks the theory of history as objective actuality. History, he says, is thought about past actuality for total actuality is chaos. The historian must make choices and the extent of his influence depends upon the correctness of his decisions. He does not exclude the scientific method but thinks that it has its limitations.

4. Becker, Carl L. "Detachment and the Writing of History" (1910), in Ten Contemporary Thinkers. Edited by Victor E. Amend and Leo T. Hendricks. New York: The Free Press of Glencoe, 1964, pp. 220-237. Originally appeared in the Atlantic Monthly, CVI (October, 1910).
Becker thinks that complete detachment in historical writing is not likely and would produce few or worthless histories since the "really detached mind is a dead mind." It is the business of the historian to arrive at concepts and to select the facts that are important for the concepts. "When old landmarks are being washed away, and old foundations are crumbling to dust, it is doubtless useful and necessary to conceive the historical reality as continuous, causally connected, and changing only in response to forces largely remote from purposive human will."

5. Becker, Carl L. "What Are Historical Facts?" in Ideas of History. Edited by Ronald H. Nash. New York: E. P. Dutton and Company, Inc., II (1969), 177-193.
Becker asks and answers three questions: What is the historical fact? Where is the historical fact? When is the

historical fact? He defines the historical fact as the affir-
mation about an event, a symbol that enables us to recreate
it imaginatively. "The historical fact is in someone's mind
or it is nowhere." The actual occurrence has passed. If
the historical fact is present, imaginatively, in someone's
mind, then it is now, a part of the present.

6. Blake, Nelson Manfred. "How to Learn History
from Sinclair Lewis and Other Unknown Sources," in American Character and Culture. Some Twentieth Century Perspectives. Edited by John A. Hague. De Land, Florida:
Everett/Edwards Press, Inc., 1964, pp. 33-47.
Blake discusses the relation of literature and other
arts--architecture, painting, music, dance--to history. He
says that the student of history must apply the same standards of historical criticism to these arts that he would
apply to other historical sources: learn about the author or
artist and why he created the work, determine the reliability
of the artist's sources, consider the probable truth or accuracy of particular statements. He says that every great
work of literature and art has both a timely quality and a
timeless quality. The historian is interested in the data that
the work reveals about the age in which it was created.
Blake applies the principles he sets up to a discussion of
Elmer Gantry as a document of social history.

7. Burnette, O. Lawrence, Jr. "Newspapers as
Historical Evidence," in Beneath the Footnote. A Guide to
the Use and Preservation of American Historical Sources.
Madison: The State Historical Society of Wisconsin, 1969,
pp. 265-284.
Burnette says that the portions of newspapers most
used by historians are editorials, illustrations, and advertise-
ments. The historian must apply the same tests to information found in newspapers that he uses to evaluate other historical material.

8. Gay, Peter. "Style in History," The American
Scholar, XLIII (Spring, 1974), 225-236.
This essay is an introduction to Gay's book, Style in
History, 1974, which centers on the style of Gibbon, Ranke,
Macaulay, and Burckhart. Since the historian is both a professional writer and a professional reader, Gay says that
the historian is under pressure to become a stylist, for he
must give pleasure as well as information. He discusses
the historian's use of various literary styles: emotional
style, professional style, and his style of thinking. Gay says

that style must be learned since writers are not born stylists
but must fashion their style through effort. "It [style] is only
in part a gift or talent; beyond that it is an act of will and
an exercise of intelligence. It is the tribute that expressive-
ness pays to discipline." Gay says that style gives access
to a writer's private, psychological world, and that study of
the style of historians provides insight into their craft or
profession as well as to culture itself.

9. Green, Constance McLaughlin. "The Value of
Local History," in The Cultural Approach to History. Edited
by Caroline F. Ware. Port Washington, N.Y.: Kennikat
Press, Inc. Copyright 1940 by Columbia University Press,
pp. 275-286.
   Green thinks that American life should be studied
from the bottom instead of from the top. Therefore the
writing and study of American local history is of primary
importance. She suggests several kinds of studies involving
local materials that would make contributions to American
cultural history. But she warns about some of the difficulties
involved in obtaining authentic local material.

10. Highet, Gilbert. "The Historian's Job," in
People, Places and Books. New York: Oxford University
Press, 1953, pp. 176-184.
   Highet says that the historian's job is to tell us about
the past, but this is a difficult if not impossible task. He
discusses three types of history: memories set down by an
eyewitness; reconstruction, a recreation from scant records;
imaginative descriptions, selection and compression of facts
from a large amount of data.

11. Kennan, George F. "The Experience of Writing
History," The Virginia Quarterly Review, XXXVI (1960),
205-214.
   Kennan discusses the difficulties encountered in writing
history: the struggle to be objective since the describing of
historical events is partly "an act of the creative imagination
of the writer"; the study and writing of history as a lonely
occupation; and the uncertainty whether what one does is worth
doing and whether it will ever be read if it is.

12. Kennan, George F. "It's History but Is It
Literature?" in Opinions and Perspectives from the New
York Times Book Review. Edited by Francis Brown. Bal-
timore, Md.: Penguin Books, Inc., 1966, pp. 386-394.
   Kennan says that a great portion of history that has

merit as science also has merit as art, for he thinks that
there is apt to be a connection between good history and
good writing. Good history, he says, can exist without good
language and style, but is used mainly for reference. It is
history as science and literature that goes beyond the
specialized reader and contributes to a general understanding
of the past. Kennan says that the kind of prose the literary
historian writes is much the same as that written by the
strictly literary person. But the historian must follow documents; he cannot create dramatic beginnings and endings;
he cannot go below the surface of men's lives but must confine himself to what is known, as distinct from what is felt.

13. Lerner, Max. "Writing 'Hot History, '" Saturday
Review, May 29, 1976, pp. 16-19.
This is a discussion of The Final Days by Robert
Woodward and Carl Bernstein as an example of "investigative
journalism" and of the value of journalism as history.
Lerner suggests five criteria for determining the line between good journalism and good history. Have the tests of
evidence been rigorously applied? Has the author tried to
make allowance for his own bias and his own value cluster?
To what extent are the returns in? What are the consequences of the events and decisions? What are the meaning
and implications of the account? Lerner says that "Unless
we know the implications of what we know, we don't know
much. That is why every good journalist-historian must
have in him at least some ingredients of the psychologist, philosopher, and social analyst, and would do well to add to the ac-
cusatory drive a brooding sense of irony and even compassion. "

14. Macaulay Thomas B. "The Writing of History, "
in "History, " Edinburgh Review, May, 1828 in Critical and
Historical Essays. Boston: Houghton Mifflin, 1900, I, 235-284.
According to Macaulay, "The perfect historian is he
in whose work the character and spirit of an age is exhibited
in miniature. " By "selection, rejection, and arrangement, "
he provides the attractions of fiction. Nothing is too insignificant if it illustrates a truth of society. Accounts of battles and affairs of government will be interspersed with
details that belong to historical romances. History written
in this manner is vivid and practical, for it appeals both to
the reason and to the imagination and helps to bring about
moral changes which are the forerunners of social revolutions.
The perfect historian must be an intellectual prodigy, a person
as scarce as Shakespeare or Homer.

15. McCoy, F. N. Researching and Writing in History. A Practical Handbook for Students. Berkeley: University of California Press, 1974. Paperback Edition. 100 pp.

A handbook, mainly for history students, organized according to the amount of time needed for each stage in the preparation of a research paper--selecting a topic, preparing the bibliography, reading and note-taking; writing, editing, and rewriting.

16. Morison, Samuel Eliot. "Faith of an Historian," The American Historical Review, LVI (January, 1951), 261-275. Reprinted in By Land and Sea. New York: Alfred A. Knopf, Inc., 1953, pp. 346-359.

In this presidential address to the American Historical Association, Morison says that a historian must have an inherent loyalty to truth, a high degree of intellectual honesty, and a sense of balance. Truth about the past is the essence of history, but the historian's sense of values will enter into his selection and arrangement of facts. The fundamental question is "What actually happened and why?" After his main object of describing events as they happened, his principle task is to understand the motives and objects of individuals and of groups, and to point out mistakes as well as achievements by persons and movements.

17. Morison, Samuel Eliot. "History as Literary Art," in By Land and Sea. New York: Alfred A. Knopf, Inc., 1953, pp. 289-298. Originally published as Old South Leaflets, Series 11, No. 1. Boston: Old South Association.

Morison says that the interest of the American reading public in historical novels rather than in history is due to the fact that historians, in their eagerness to present facts, have forgotten that there is an art of writing history. Historians have regarded history as a science and have written history that is boring to the reader. Morison makes a plea for Ph.D.'s to write histories that people care to read. He advises the young historian or graduate student to concentrate on improvement in craftsmanship. He makes the following suggestions: Begin writing and continue writing as long as you can without stopping to consult notes. Do not bother to verify facts and quotations. After the words are on paper, return to the notes and compose the next few pages or paragraphs. Try to achieve clarity, vigor, and objectivity. Always keep the reader in mind and do not be afraid to rewrite. Read your paper aloud to test for interest, for clarity, and for improving the language. He thinks that the writer can improve his style and clarify his thinking by reading Latin and Greek authors, either in the original or in good translations, and English classics and novels, especially the novels of Henry James. The writer can also use his imagination to weave facts into a pattern if he makes clear what is fact and what is hypothesis.

18. Nevins, Allan. "Literary Aspects of History," in The Gateway to History. Revised Edition. Garden City, N.Y.: Doubleday and Company, Inc., Anchor Books, 1962, pp. 371-391.
Nevins says that the "ideal in history is a work on which infinite labor has first been expended to obtain and utilize the materials, and infinite pains have then been expended to hide the labor." Such effort allows the historian to convert the material into a harmonious whole and to release his imagination and his reflective powers. Nevins says there is no real conflict between literary and scientific history since it is possible to be scientific and exact and also to write with literary charm. Readers, he thinks, prefer literary charm to scientific solidity.

19. Nichols, Roy F. "Genealogy: A Historian's Hobby," in A Historian's Progress. New York: Alfred A. Knopf, Inc., 1968, pp. 189-198.
An account of Nichols's work in tracing his ancestry.

20. Parker, Donald Dean. Local History. How to Gather It, Write It, and Publish It. Revised and Edited by Bertha E. Josephson. New York: Social Science Research Council, 1944. 186 pp.
This book was written for students, teachers, and adults not connected with educational institutions and is thus a practical guide for writing local history. Part I is concerned with gathering material. Part II gives concrete aids in writing local history. Part III discusses various means of publishing local history.

21. Schlesinger, Arthur M., Jr. "The Historian as Artist," Atlantic, CCXII (July, 1963), 35-41.
Schlesinger says that written history "is the application of an aesthetic vision to a welter of facts; and both the weight and the vitality of a historical work depend on the quality of the vision." Although technical history, he says, has made contributions to the writing of history, it has caused history to lose its popularity with the reading public.

But the renunciation of the technical historian has led to the
rise of the "prophetic" historian who indulges in dogmatic
historical theories. Schlesinger's solution to the present
dilemma of historians is for the historian to be not only a
researcher and an analyzer but a literary artist as well.

22. Schlesinger, Arthur M., Jr. "On the Writing of
Contemporary History," Atlantic, CC (March, 1967), 69-74.
Schlesinger discusses the effect of the use of the type-
writer and the telephone on documents available to the modern
historian and the ways by which the modern historian can improve the record for the historian of the future. He mentions
particularly the contributions of oral history interviews and
he raises the question as to how far the persons being interviewed can control the material and to what extent the contemporary historian should enter into the private lives of the
figures with whom he deals. He thinks that contemporary
history must be even more exacting in its standards than the
history of the past since it can be contradicted by actual
participants. He says that it may well be that the contemporary historian understands better what is going on than
will historians who will write of the events at a later time.

23. Stegner, Wallace. "On the Writing of History,"
in The Sound of Mountain Water. Garden City, N.Y.:
Doubleday and Company, Inc., 1969, pp. 202-222.
Stegner discusses the similarities between history and
fiction and illustrates his remarks by referring to the writing
of four of his own books--a history, a biography, a history
with novelistic emphasis, a combination of reminiscence and
fiction--and to the correspondence of Bernard DeVoto and
Garrett Mattingly, both of whom believed that "transforma-
tion of fact by the imagination" is the highest reach of the
historian's art.

24. Toynbee, Arnold J. "Why and How I Work," in
Experiences. New York: Oxford University Press, 1969,
pp. 87-105.
Toynbee offers five pieces of advice to intellectual
workers: think before you act and give yourself time to see
your project as a whole; do not wait too long before plunging
in; write regularly whether you feel inclined to write or not;
do not waste odd pieces of time; always look ahead, for you
may keep notes that you will want to use later on.

25. Trevelyan, George Macaulay. "Bias in History,"
in An Autobiography and Other Essays. Longmans, Green

and Company, Ltd., 1949. Freeport, N.Y.: Books for
Libraries Press, 1971, pp. 68-81.
　　　Trevelyan thinks that bias in history is not necessarily either good or bad. He defines it as "any personal
interpretation of historical events which is not acceptable to
the whole human race." He thinks there are two functions
of the writer or teacher of history: to show the consequences
of actions in the past and to relate them to later times, and
to find out what people of the past themselves thought and
felt. He raises the question of whether the historian should
be biased in favor of morality. He thinks that true history
can only do good and that false history only makes for
fanaticism and war. Even true history cannot exist with
bias. A historian should be a philosopher, a wise man, who
has the right kind of bias.

　　　26. Trevelyan, George Macaulay. "Clio, a Muse,"
in Clio, a Muse and Other Essays, 1930. Freeport, N.Y.:
Books for Libraries Press, 1968, pp. 140-176.
　　　Trevelyan raises three questions about history:
Should history be merely the accumulations of facts about
the past? Should it also include interpretation of facts about
the past? Should it not also be the exposition of these facts
and opinions in their full emotional and intellectual value by
the art of literature? He concludes that history is only in
part a matter of "fact," and that the most important part of
its business is not scientific deduction but an imaginative
guess at the most likely generalizations. The main purpose
of history, he says, is educative. This is accomplished in
several ways: by training the mind of the citizens so that
they are capable of taking a just view of political problems;
by helping to remove prejudice and generating enthusiasm
for improving society; by enabling the reader to understand
the historical aspects of literature; and by adding to the enjoyment of travel. He thinks that the art of history is in
the art of narrative.

　　　27. Tuchman, Barbara W. "The Historian as
Artist," New York Herald Tribune, 1966. Reprinted in The
Writer, February, 1968, pp. 15-17, 46.
　　　Tuchman says that the historian is a creative writer,
an artist on the same level as that of the poet or novelist.
She thinks that there are three parts to the creative process:
the vision by which the artist perceives and conveys truth,
the medium of expression (language of writers), and design
or structure. Writing good clear prose is hard work and
historical structure requires arrangement, composition,

planning. Other problems peculiar to writing history are
explaining background without interfering with the story and
creating suspense and maintaining interest in a story of
which the outcome is well known.

28. Tuchman, Barbara W. "The Historian's Opportunity," Saturday Review, L (January-March, 1967), 27-31,
71. Reprinted in The Saturday Review Fiftieth Anniversary
Reader. Edited by Richard L. Tobin and S. Spencer Grin.
New York: Bantam Books, 1974, pp. 125-144.
Tuchman says that the current decline of the novel as
well as of poetry and drama has turned the interest of the
reading public to the literature of actuality. Thus the historian may become the major interpreter in literary experience of man's role in society, to tell what human history is
about and what the forces are that drive us. But in order
to share its insights with the public, history must communicate with its members. The other elements of history are
research, which provides the material, and theory, which
presents a pattern of thought; but it is through communication
that history influences.

29. Webb, Walter Prescott. "History as High Ad-
venture," American Historical Review, LXIV (January, 1959),
265-281. Reprinted in An Honest Preface and Other Essays
by Walter Prescott Webb, with an appreciative introduction
by Joe B. Frantz. Boston: Houghton Mifflin Company,
1959, pp. 194-216.
In this presidential address before the American Historical Association, Webb tells how he became a historian.
He explains how he gathered material and wrote four books:
The Great Plains, 1931, regional; The Texas Rangers, 1935,
local; Divided We Stand, 1936, national; and The Great
Frontier, 1952, international. "Taken together they tell the
story of the expansion of the mind from a hard-packed West
Texas dooryard to the outer limits of the Western World."

30. Wecter, Dixon. "History and How to Write It,"
American Heritage, VIII (August, 1957), 24-27, 87.
Wecter defines history as "a review of the success and
failure of man's life on this planet." He warns historians
against the abuse of history by being dull and imaginative, by
being careless in handling facts, by a desire to be shocking,
or by using history as propaganda. History, he says, helps
to destroy prejudice and hatred between races, sections, and
national groups. Wecter suggests that since history is both
a science and an art, that "horse sense, independence, and

strict integrity are vital to the good writing of good history.
There must be "exact knowledge fired by historical imagination."

31.   Wedgwood, C. V.   "The Historian and the
World," in Velvet Studies.   London: Jonathan Cape, 1946,
pp. 154-159.   Originally published in Time and Tide,
November 12 and 21, 1942.
   Wedgwood says that there are two kinds of writers
concerned with history: the scholars and the popularizers.
The scholars are interested in uncovering material, not in
its ultimate use.   The popularizers make the material
palatable to the public and thus have in their power the
means of influencing society.   For this reason Wedgwood
thinks that it is the business of historical writers "to draw
morals," for if the judicious fail to do so, the unscrupulous
will do it for them.   "A nation does not create the history
it deserves; the historians are far more likely to create the
nation."   The historian's first duty, she says, is not to his
subject but to his audience.   That is why the historian shou
be a good man.

32.   White, Lynn T., Jr.   "History and Horseshoe
Nails," in The Historian's Workshop.   Original Essays by
Sixteen Historians.   Edited by L. P. Curtin, Jr.   New
York: Alfred A. Knopf, 1970, pp. 49-64.
   An account of how White became interested in researching and writing about medieval technology and the
areas into which his research led him.   History, to White,
is not merely written records but "even the subliminal elements of life in the past."

33.   Williamson, Samuel T.   "How to Write Like a
Social Scientist," Saturday Review of Literature, XXX
(October 4, 1947), 17, 27-28.
   A criticism of the writing of economists, sociologist
and authorities on government, who, Williamson says, follo
six rules in their writing: use long words when a short
word would suffice; use many long words; use polysyllabic
words; explain the obvious in terms of the unintelligible;
announce what is to be said before saying it; defend their
style as scientific.

34.   Woodham-Smith, Cecil.   "Writing History Is
Nervous Work," in Opinions and Perspectives from The Nev
York Times Book Review.   Edited by Francis Brown.   Bal:
more, Md.:   Penguin Books, Inc., 1966, pp. 361-366.

Writing history is nervous work since there are so many historians eager to find mistakes in the writing, and accuracy is the criterion for judging the historian's work. Some of the pitfalls that Cecil Woodham-Smith warns the writer against in gathering material are the failure to recognize that two persons may use the same initials as signatures, that there may be two persons by the same name, that the "second creation" of titles in England may confuse, that place names are often repeated, and that the use of capital or small letters may be indicative.

WRITING ASSIGNMENTS

1. Kennan mentions in "It's History but Is It Literature?" that in writing about Russia in the period of the Russian civil war of 1918 to 1920, he was concerned with what happened to men in their political and social dealings with one another, and in Doctor Zhivago, which deals with the same period, Pasternak was concerned with revealing what happened to individuals in their reactions to these events. Read the two accounts and write a paper in which you compare the material and the method used by these two writers.

2. In his book on the writing of local history, Parker lists twenty local sources that a writer of local history might use in searching for material: family histories, anniversary addresses and sermons, photographs, cemeteries, interviews with older residents, newspapers and periodicals, census reports, etc. Select a topic relating to your own locality, and using local material, write a paper presenting what you find. You may use such topics as "Local Place Names and History of the Community," "Here a Battle Was Fought," "The Oldest House in Town," "Indian Mounds and History."

3. Read the article by Roy F. Nichols, "Genealogy: A Historian's Hobby," and write a paper in which you describe your own ancestry. Examine family records, and obtain information in interviews with older members of the family, from local civil and religious records, and from records in libraries of historical and genealogical societies.

4. Select a short piece of good historical writing and write a paper in which you show why the writing is good historical writing. Examine the sources, the organization, and the method of writing. You may use one of the following selections:

     a. Carlyle, Thomas. "The Steeples at Midnight," in The French Revolution. New York: Random House. Modern Library Edition, pp. 454-460.

     b. Durant, Will and Ariel. "Rousseau Wanderer," in Rousseau and Revolution. New York: Simon and Schuster, 1967, pp. 3-5.

     c. Miller, John. "The Battle of Trenton," in Triumph of Freedom. Boston: Little, Brown and Company, 1948, pp. 153-162.

     d. Tuchman, Barbara. "A Funeral," in The Guns of August. New York: Macmillan Company, 1962, pp. 1-14.

     e. White, Theodore H. "Episode in Tokyo Bay," Atlantic Monthly, CCXXVI (July-December, 1970), pp. 53-59.

5. Archaeology is another source of history. Visit an archaeological museum in your community, or a local excavation such as that of an Indian mound, and write a paper in which you discuss the history revealed by the articles that you find. You may want to read such books as Gods, Graves, and Scholars. The Story of Archaeology by C. W. Ceram, 1952; The First American. A Story of North American Archaeology by C. W. Ceram, 1971; Southwestern Archaeology by John C. McGregor, Second Edition, 1965.

6. Write a paper in which you discuss methods used for determining dates--such as tree-ring dates; the location and form of plants; use of scientific instruments and radiocarbon dating; markings on pottery; architecture; burial customs; weapons; etc. Where possible, provide examples of your statements.

7. Trevelyan says in "Clio, a Muse," that modern historical writing is weakest in narrative, a weakness that he thinks is "spinal." Select a history and examine it for its "art of narrative," and then write a paper showing wherein it is weak or strong in this respect.

8. Select two histories that give opposite viewpoints of the same subject and write a paper in which you point out the differences. Try to account for the differences and to assess the effect of the biased viewpoints on a correct presentation of the situation. Histories concerned with the Revolutionary Period, the Civil War, and World War II may offer good material for such a study. You may also want to mention historians who give fair appraisals in their works.

9. In "Writing 'Hot History, '" Max Lerner mentions When the Cheering Stopped, an account of the last days of Woodrow Wilson, by Gene Smith, 1964, as an example of good history as well as of good journalism. Read the book and write a paper in which you discuss both aspects of the work.

10. In "Writing 'Hot History, '" Lerner says, "The craft of history is always in need of rebarbarizing by the energies of talented amateurs, lest it come under the dictatorship of the mandarins." Using such books as When the Cheering Stopped, All the President's Men, and The Final Days, write a paper in which you discuss the contributions that journalists have made to history.

"All history becomes subjective; in other words there is properly no history, only biography."

--Ralph W. Emerson, "History," The Complete Essays and Other Writings of Ralph Waldo Emerson. Introduction by Brooks Atkinson. Modern Library College Edition. New York: Random House, 1950, p. 127.

"The writing of biography involves, as does no other form of non-fiction, a combination of science and art. Biography is a bridge between history and the novel, combining the historian's method of research and his respect for truth with the novelist's concern for writing as an art and his interest in the convincing portrayal of a human character."

--John A. Garraty, "How to Write a Biography," The South Atlantic Quarterly, LV (January, 1956), 73.

"By telling us true facts, by sifting the little from the big, and shaping the whole so that we perceive the outline, the biographer does more to stimulate the imagination than any poet or novelist save the very greatest. For few poets and novelists are capable of that high degree of tension which gives us much more than another fact to add to our collection. He can give us the creative fact; the fertile fact; the fact that suggests and engenders."

--Virginia Woolf, "The Art of Biography," Atlantic Monthly, CLXIII (1939), 510.

BIOGRAPHY AND AUTOBIOGRAPHY

The problems that biographers face are concerned with locating and evaluating materials, with deciding how to handle delicate information about their subjects, with how much interpretation the biographer may apply to the facts, with how far he may use Freudian techniques, and with the form and structure the biography will take. The autobiographer has many of the same problems, but he also has to guard against non-objectivity and inventiveness. There is also much discussion by writers of biography as to whether the biographer is an artist or a craftsman, and whether biography is history or should include some of the elements of fiction. Attention is also given to the importance of making the biography interesting to the reader.

1. Adams, James Truslow. "Biography as an Art," in The Tempo of Modern Life. First published 1931. Freeport N.Y.: Books for Libraries Press, Essay Reprint Series, 1970, pp. 187-199.
Adams discusses the merits of two kinds of biography: to teach by example and "to transmit a personality." The biographers of the first group, he says, have their data fairly sharply defined. The writers of the second group must decide what constitutes a personality and thus what constitutes man; that is, what are the human qualities of the highest worth. Adams says that his examination of biographies of recent years shows that the selection of material has been based mainly on the part of the hero's career in which he departs from the accepted mores, a practice that he considers absurd since the mores change. In fact, he says that many current biographers distort the picture by showing their heroes of the past departing from the mores of today. He says that the test should be whether the facts in question had any lasting influence on the man, his career, and personality. He thinks that only recorded facts should be

used and that the biographer's appreciation of the subject's character should not serve as a substitute for facts. "A superb biographer may play the artist; an ordinary craftsman had better play the photographer of the obvious."

2. Anthony, Katharine. "Writing Biography," in The Writer's Book. Edited by Helen Hull. New York: Harper, 1950, pp. 220-226.
Anthony says that the biographer combines the methods of the novelist, the research of the scholar, and the accuracy of the historian. "The cleanliness, simplicity, and rectitude of his original facts are the biographer's best assurance of the final integrity of his work." He must absorb much history for which he has no immediate use, and the historical background of the life he is presenting should be mapped out in his mind, but the life-likeness of the central character is the primary aim of the biographer.

3. Atlas, James. "Literary Biography," The American Scholar, (Summer, 1976), pp. 448, 450-456, 458-460.
Atlas says that biography has never been securely established as a genre, a situation that has led several practitioners to publish theories of their work. He discusses the work and the theories of Leon Edel, Richard Ellmann, and A. O. J. Cockshut; of Lytton Strachey and of Virginia Woolf; of George Painter's Proust in relation to Edel's Henry James and Ellmann's James Joyce; and of Mark Schorer's Sinclair Lewis, John Unterecker's Voyager: A Life of Hart Crane, Louis Shaeffer's biography of Eugene O'Neill, Joseph Blotner's two-volume of William Faulkner, and R. W. Stallman's biography of Stephen Crane. He concludes: "Until biographers recognize the limits of documentation as a means of yielding truth, biography will continue to relinquish the claim it once had as a literary form."

4. Biography as an Art. Selected Criticism, 1560-1960. Edited by James L. Clifford, New York: Oxford University Press, 1962. Galaxy Edition. 256 pp.
A collection of essays by biographers of the following periods: Before 1700, The Eighteenth Century, The Nineteenth Century, Early Twentieth Century, Mid-Twentieth Century. An appendix provides an additional list of twentieth-century publications containing criticisms of biography.

5. Bowen, Catherine Drinker. Adventures of a Biographer. Boston: Little, Brown and Company, 1959. 235 pp.

Although not directed to writers, this book is an exciting account of the business of writing biography. "Like courtship, it [writing biography] has its moments of gratification and its days of despair, when history closes her doors and will not show her face." The fourteen chapters are concerned with some of the problems Bowen encountered in writing biography, the people she met in her research travels, her experience with college professors of history, and the aid she received from librarians.

6. Bowen, Catherine Drinker. Biography: The Craft and the Calling. Boston: Little, Brown and Company, 1969. 174 pp.
This book is concerned with how a biographer puts his book together and the ways and means of writing it. The fifteen chapters treat such topics as plotting the biography, shaping the biography, beginning and ending the biography, the biographer's relation to his character, the perils and pleasures of research, the importance of the preface. Bowen says that technique is teachable, but that talent can only be discovered and encouraged. The concluding chapter is a collection of statements about talent and genius made by "the great and the near great."

7. Bowen, Catherine Drinker. "The Business of a Biographer," Atlantic Monthly, CLXXXVII (May 1951), 50-56.
Bowen says that it is the business of a historian to be exciting and it is even more so for the biographer, for biography is more immediately comprehensible. She tells how she became interested in writing about John Adams, how she did research for her book, John Adams and the Revolution, what her purpose was in writing the book, and why she chose the form she used. She describes the schedule she set herself for reading, for collecting material, and for writing the book. She allowed herself two full years for reading, twelve months in which to work out the order of her narrative, and twenty-four months in which to write.

8. Bowen, Elizabeth. "Autobiography as an Art," The Saturday Review of Literature, XXXIV (March 17, 1951), 9-10.
Elizabeth Bowen says that modern autobiography is a product of "disciplined concentration." It is a combination of the writer's individual and social background and his "visionary element," an expression of the writer's attitudes and temperament. Modern autobiographies are often the work of early or late maturity and the writers speak not only for themselves

but for their contemporaries. The secret of the modern
interest in autobiography, thinks Bowen, is that it has become an art, for it involves choice of material, order,
thought, and feeling. "Autobiography as we know it now is
artists' work; though pegged to one man's story it has for
its subject Life, as by one man that has been found to be.
The findings may not be ours; the subject is."

9. Chute, Marchette. "Getting at the Truth," The
Saturday Review, XXXVI (September 19, 1953), 11-12, 43-44.
Chute says that a biographer will never succeed in
getting at the truth if he thinks he knows in advance what the
truth ought to be. She warns the biographer that attention
must be given to the point of view of the writer of the information as well as to what he has written, and he must
realize that being objective is difficult. She says that the
point of view and the frame of reference in a biography must
be implicit in the material and should not be imposed upon it.

10. Clifford, James L. "The Complex Art of Biography
or All the Doctor Johnsons," Columbia University Forum, 1958,
pp. 32-37. Repr. in Academic Discourse. Ed., John J. Enck.
New York: Appleton-Century-Crofts, 1964, pp. 189-197.
The writing of biography is "complex" because of
many factors: the biographer must choose from many statements, all of them not of equal validity; the biographer has
an emotional response to the person he is describing, a situation that complicates the picture he presents; evidence must
be interpreted by the biographer, but he is limited in amplification since the biography may become fiction; the biographer
may have to reckon with different accounts of the same episode; the twentieth-century biographer must decide how much
to use psychological techniques; often there are instances
where logic will not suffice and the biographer's total con-
cept of his subject must be the deciding factor.

11. Clifford, James L. From Puzzles to Portraits.
Problems of a Literary Biographer. Chapel Hill: The University of North Carolina Press, 1970. 151 pp.
Clifford, a practicing biographer, tells of the problems
of research and the excitement of uncovering biographical material by being at the right place at the right time. In "Part
One. Finding the Evidence," he discusses the importance of
locating original material--letters, diaries, manuscripts, etc.
--since material edited before the twentieth century cannot be
trusted for accuracy. In this section, he relates stories of
his own experiences in locating original material in England

and Wales. Part Two is concerned with how the biographer
evaluates the reliability of his assembled facts, with the
various types of biography with the problem of the biographer
in choosing the material to use, and with the problem of deciding "how much" of the subject's life a biographer should
tell.

12. Cockshut, A. O. J. "A Neglected Form," in
Truth to Life. The Art of Biography in the Nineteenth
Century. New York: Harcourt Brace Jovanovich, 1974,
pp. 11-15.
Cockshut thinks that a biography should be judged on
its accuracy as history before it can be considered as a work
of art. The main difficulty of biography as art, he thinks,
lies mainly in the tension between interpretation and facts.
But facts alone are not biography. The hardest tactical
problem is that of time; that is, the biographer should show
his subject as he "dreams and broods and hopes." He should
show his memories and his regrets. The second tactical
difficulty is that an interpretation is apt to be over-simplified
since there is always something not accounted for.

13. Cox, James M. "Autobiography and America,"
in Aspects of Narrative. Selected Papers from The English
Institute. Edited by J. Hillis Miller. New York and London:
Columbia University Press, 1971, pp. 143-172.
Cox says that autobiography falls between history and
fictive narrative in that it deals with fact and is concerned
with the representation of persons. He uses Franklin's Autobiography, Thoreau's Walden, Adams's The Education of
Henry Adams, and Gertrude Stein's The Autobiography of
Alice B. Toklas to illustrate his views of good autobiographi-
cal writing in America.

14. Edel, Leon. Literary Biography. The Alexander
Lectures, 1955-56. Toronto: The University of Toronto
Press, 1957. 113 pp.
A series of five lectures concerned with aspects of the
writing about men and women who were themselves writers.
Edel offers certain general considerations about the biographer
and his subject, and discusses the search for materials, the
problem of weighing the relationship between criticism and
biography, the use of psychology and psycho-analysis by the
biographer, and the actual writing of the biography. "All
biography," Edel says, "is, in effect a kind of semi-scientific
and historical form of the inert materials, re-assembled, so
to speak, through the mind of the historian or biographer.
He becomes the informing mind. He can only lay bare the

facts as he understood them." Edel says that there are at
least three ways of structuring biographies: the traditional
documentary biography in which the biographer arranges the
materials ("chronicle"), the creation in words of a kind of
painter's portrait ("pictorial"), the biography in which the
biographer is present as an omniscient narrator ("narrative-
pictorial or novelistic").

15. Edel, Leon. "That One May Say This Was the
Man," in Opinions and Perspectives from The New York
Times Book Review. Edited by Francis Brown. Baltimore,
Md.: Penguin Books, Inc., 1966, pp. 423-427.
Edel says that the biographer may use his imagination
in bringing materials together, but he must tell the truth and
not re-create a life in his own image. The twentieth-century
biographer must use a wealth of documentary material and he
must be careful not to distort by choice of material, but he
must evaluate and interpret facts so that he may present a
reasonable likeness of the character he is describing.

16. Edel, Leon. "Time and the Biographer," New
Republic, CXXXII (February 21, 1955), 19-21.
Edel says that biography, especially literary biography,
has been too much concerned with facts and not sufficiently
concerned with recreating the life of the person written about.
He thinks that "biographers should remind themselves that a
life they are writing about was not a series of facts on cards
but was once filled with feeling and with poetry, with moments
of light and moments of darkness, with brooding despair and
also exultation." Since the modern biographer has access to
a mass of documents, one of his problems is to restore a
"time-sense" to the material so that the reader has a sense
of a life lived. Edel disagrees with Maurois, who thinks that
a biography must be chronological. He thinks that the biographer should find in documents not only what happened but
what everything that happened meant to his subject. Much of
this may be found in the writer's own work.

17. Ellmann, Richard. "Literary Biography," in
Golden Codgers: Biographical Speculations. New York: Oxford University Press, 1973, pp. 1-16.
Ellmann is concerned with the problems that biographers
face at the present time, for, he says, we want in modern
biography to see the character forming rather than already
formed. This involves the use of Freudian techniques. He
illustrates his statements by referring to the biographies of
Baudelaire, Genet, and Flaubert; Erik Erikson's study of Young

Martin Luther; Leon Edel's biography of Henry James; and
George Painter's post-Freudian biography of Proust. Ell-
man concludes that although biography uses experiments
comparable to those of the novel and poem, it still must retain a chronological pattern. "Biographies," he says, "will
continue to be archival, but the best ones will offer speculations, conjectures, hypotheses." He anticipates that the
future biographer may approach his subject at different levels,
and he thinks that the attempt to understand how a mind works
when it is producing literature is a worthwhile undertaking.

18. Garraty, John A. "How to Write a Biography,"
The South Atlantic Quarterly, LV (January, 1956), 73-86.
Expanded in The Nature of Biography. New York: Alfred A.
Knopf, 1956, pp. 241-259.
Garraty says that biography is a bridge between history
and the novel. He shows that there is no one way to write a
biography by presenting the methods used by the following
biographers: Katherine Anthony, Joseph Hergesheimer, Isaak
Walton, James F. Stanfield, Charlotte Buehler, James Parton,
Henry Adams, Harold Nicolson, Hesketh Pearson, Stefan
Zweig, Catherine Drinker Bowen, Carl Sandburg, Albert J.
Beveridge, Gordon W. Allport, and Mallory Trent.

19. Herold, Christopher. "The Biographer at Work,"
in The Quest for Truth. Compiled by Martha Boaz. New
York: The Scarecrow Press, Inc., 1961, pp. 59-77.
The difficulty of the biographer's work begins with the
choice of a subject, which in turn determines the methods to
be applied. There must also be some sympathy between the
biographer and his subject. It is best to choose a person as
subject who has made more of his life than has the average
person, who has left personal documents, and who has lived
in a time not very remote from that of the writer. The form
for the biography must come from the material. The biographer must read everything that has been written on his subject as well as articles and books that the subject has written.
Herold does not believe in taking extensive notes and in waiting
to finish reading before beginning to write. The biographer
should "never take anything for granted; never to gloss over
any difficulties, contradictions, or gaps, and never to cease
asking oneself the same questions in every paragraph one
writes: When? How? Where? Who? and so forth." The
result of a biographer's labors should be an "uncluttered and
harmonious whole."

20. Howarth, William L. "Some Principles of

Autobiography," New Literary History, V (Winter, 1974), 363-381.

An autobiography, according to Howarth, is a self-portrait, equally a work of art and of life. In autobiography "vision and memory remain the essential controls, time and space the central problems, reduction and expansion the desired goals." Since in writing his story, the autobiographer shapes his life into an artful pattern, an autobiography is not entirely factual, unimaginative, or non-fictional. Howarth lists the elements of autobiography as character, which must be distinguished from the author; technique, which includes style, imagery, structure; and theme, which expresses the writer's general attitudes and links him to his reader. He says that autobiography falls into three groups: autobiography as oratory, in which group he places St. Augustine, John Bunyan, Edward Gibbon, Henry Adams, and Malcolm X; autobiography as drama, which stresses spectacle and the visible aspects of life, as shown by such writers as Cellini, Boswell, Franklin, Pepys, and Mark Twain; and autobiography as poetry, which includes such writers as Rousseau, Thoreau, Whitman, Yeats, Agee, Goethe, Wordsworth, and Henry James.

21. Lewis, Wilmarth S. "The Difficult Art of Biography," The Yale Review, XLIV (Autumn, 1954), 33-40.
Lewis quotes Sir Harold Nicolson as saying that a biography must be an accurate history of an individual in relation to his time; it must describe an individual; and it must be written as a branch of literature. Lewis says that an author who is writing about a contemporary has certain advantages: he can interview his subject and members of his family, friends, and enemies; he knows how his subject dressed, walked, ate, and spoke; he knows the times in which his subject lived. The best biographers are able to break through the time barrier. The noncontemporary biographer has the advantage of perspective and he is free to say what he likes without regard to the feelings of living persons. The chief disadvantage that all biographers share is ignorance of what actually took place in the character's life. "Biography demands much of its practitioners: study, accuracy, insight, and artistry."

22. Nevins, Allan. "The Autobiography," in Allan Nevins on History. Compiled and Introduced by Ray Allen Billington. New York: Charles Scribner's Sons, 1975, pp. 236-246.
The writing of autobiography, says Nevins, requires more care than the writing of biography. There are several

reasons: a truthful record requires self-knowledge and candor; memory is not always reliable; the writer must have a proper sense of proportion to handle a mass of material; the writer is apt to remember the past as being better than it was. Nevins describes a large number of published autobiographies and explains what each shows about the character of the writer.

23. Nevins, Allan. "The Essence of Biography," in Allan Nevins on History. Compiled and Introduced by Ray Allen Billington. New York: Charles Scribner's Sons, 1975, pp. 217-235.
Nevins says that it is the creative element in any kind of writing that makes it great. The creative element is identical for the biography and the novel. The ways of identifying greatness in both novels and biographies are: the creation of characters that live, and a story that relates the character to the laws of human experience. Nevins suggests that the biographer think of layers of human personality and character: the outward layer of physical features, speech, ways of acting and talking; the taste of the man in books and friends; the elements of character known only to his closest associates; his conduct shown by some great crisis.

24. Nicolson, Harold. "How I Write Biography," The Saturday Review of Literature, X (May 26, 1934), 709-711.
Biography is the history of the life of an individual written as a branch of literature. As history, it must be true. In that it describes an individual, it must be personal. In that it is a branch of literature, it must be written with regard to construction, balance, and style. The biographer is not obliged to tell the whole truth if it disturbs the proposition of his work. Nicolson says that he works according to the following principle: "If a biographer discovers material which is so sensational and shocking that it will disturb not only the average reader, but the whole proportions of his own work, then he is justified in suppressing the actual facts. He is not justified, however, in suppressing the conclusions which he himself draws from those facts, and he must alter his portrait so that it conforms to those facts."

25. Nicolson, Harold. "The Practice of Biography," American Scholar, XXIII (1954), 151-161. Originally published in The Cornhill Magazine.
Nicolson defines a "pure" biography as one that is accurate, that depicts an individual in relation to his time, and

is written with some attention to style. The biographer
should not let his own personality intrude upon that of the
personality he is describing. He must not use the techniques
of fiction or romance to color his narrative. He recommends that the biographer select a subject within his range
of sympathy or general knowledge, and he should not conceal
defects but put them in proper perspective. A pure biography, according to Nicolson, "can only be written about a
person whom the reader and the writer can fundamentally
respect."

    26. Nock, Albert Jay. "The Purpose of Biography,"
Atlantic Monthly, CLXV (1940), 340-346.
    Nock says that the function of modern biography is to
help the historian, but the writing of sophisticated biography
is bad since it includes material of no historical significance
and fosters the idea that knowing about a subject is the same
thing as knowing the subject. Nock refers to the autobiography of Rimsky-Korsakov as a good example of how the account of a life should include only information that bears on
the purpose of the book, in this case, the author's character
and activities as a musician, as a means of helping the historian of Russian music. Additional merits of the book are
its objectivity and the precise way in which it is written.

    27. Origo, Iris. "Biography, True and False,"
Atlantic Monthly, CCIII (February, 1959), 38-42.
    Origo mentions three temptations that the biographer
faces: to suppress, to invent, and to sit in judgment. She
agrees with Dr. Johnson that the whole truth should be told,
for "It keeps mankind from despair." She thinks that the
biographer who condescends to his subject ends by writing
more about himself than about his subject. Although the
judgment of character is the central problem of biography,
the biographer should be careful not to smother his subject
with his own ideas. Her advice to the young biographer is
to let his material produce its own effect, "to listen without
interrupting," and he may come near to the truth of what
another man was like and through him, understand man in
the abstract.

    28. Partington, Wilfred. "Should a Biographer
Tell?" Atlantic Monthly, CLXXX (August, 1947), 56-63.
    Partington says that the real historians are the
biographers, autobiographers, and diarists. But good biographers are few since they are reticent about telling the
complete story of a person's life. They are also subject to

libel if they write about delicate matters while the persons
are still living. Thus there is a tendency among modern
biographers to leave unpleasant facts alone. He illustrates
his statement that biographers are failing to do their job
honestly by referring to an article in the Dictionary of
American Biography, a publication concerned only with historical fact, that fails to give the complete story of the fraud
committed by Thomas Powell, a contemporary of Charles
Dickens.

29. Reid, B. L. "Practical Biography," Sewanee
Review, LXXXIII (Spring, 1975), 357-363.
Reid opposes the idea that biography is a branch of
the fine arts. He considers biography a mode of history
and a useful and a necessary art. Its basic function, he
thinks, is that of "truthful chronicle, of the ordering of facts
within the discipline of time." It should be well written, but
it should not try to be a novel. It should be selective and
the material should determine the shape.

30. Schorer, Mark. "The Burdens of Biography,"
in To the Young Writer. Edited by A. L. Bader. Ann
Arbor: The University of Michigan Press. Ann Arbor Paperbacks, 1965, pp. 147-165.
In writing biography, Schorer says that one must confine himself to facts, but "facts can be surprisingly friendly,
and they have not infrequently, an eloquence, even a kind of
poetry, that may well go far beyond the inventions of imagination." There are problems in using living witnesses, for
they may be reticent, want to dress up the occasion, be
partisan in view, or be mistaken in their memories. Personal
intimacy with one's subject has certain disadvantages: obliga-
tions to friendship may distort the facts or lead to a mere
memoir. Schorer distinguishes among the drudge, who can
only compile material in a chronological catalogue; the critic,
who must analyze; and the artist, who can not only bring
order out of a mass of material but give it living shape so
that his subject lives in the "reanimated history of his time."
Schorer says that all of the principles that pertain to fiction
pertain to proper biography, but he warns against the biographer trying to psychoanalyze his subject.

31. Smith, Bradford. "Biographer's Creed," William
and Mary Quarterly, XX (April, 1953), 190-195.
The biographer should use the techniques of the historian to get facts and the devices of the novelist to appeal to
a general audience. He can use dialogue, description, analysis,

narrative, and he must know the society in which his subject lived. "The historian is interested in recreating the past for his own time; the biographer recreates the personality of the individual through whom the times live." Biography, says Smith, is "life-writing." It is history relived on the human scale. To the extent that the biographer feels what his subject felt and presents it so that the reader also feels it, biography is autobiography. Biography "completes the circle of meaning--from subject to author to reader to universal."

32. Tolles, Frederick B. "The Biographer's Craft," The South Atlantic Quarterly, LIII (1954), 508-520.
Tolles refers to his biography of George Logan to illustrate his ideas about how a biography should be written. The biographer must learn to write narrative; he must show rather than tell; he must keep his main character in the spotlight; he must limit background material to the barest minimum; he must not speculate but must use facts; he must write about the character and not about the sources of information about the character; he must give to his biography a shape, a form, "something added by the shaping spirit of the artist"; he must use his imagination; he must practice an art that conceals scholarship, not the lack of it.

33. Woodress, James. "The Writing of Biography," in The Quest for Truth, II. The Continuing Quest. Compiled by Martha Boaz. Metuchen, N.J.: The Scarecrow Press, Inc., 1967, pp. 82-96.
Woodress says that the "legwork" connected with writing a biography is more interesting than the writing, for there is always the excitement of uncovering new material. The biographer must have in mind the image of his reader and he needs to have a detailed chronology of his subject. He says that he concentrates on the significant aspects of his subject's life and then tries to relate the important events with the subject's everyday life. Woodress illustrates his statements by referring to his writing of the biographies of Booth Tarkington and Joel Barlow.

34. Writing About Oneself. Selected Writing. Edited by Robert Garis. Boston: D. C. Heath, 1965. Paperback Edition. 143 pp.
Selected examples of mainly autobiographical writing from important writers. Section I, "Memory, Nostalgia and Sentimentality," includes selections of childhood memories from Agee, Lawrence, Hopkins, Wordsworth, Nabokov, Tolstoy, and Joyce; Section II, "Confession and Self-Deception,"

has selections from Rousseau, Dostoyevsky, Orwell, Mc-
Carthy, and Dennis.

35. Woolf, Virginia. "The Art of Biography," in
Collected Essays, IV. New York: Harcourt, Brace and
World, Inc., 1925-1967, pp. 221-228. Originally published
in Atlantic Monthly, CLXIII (1939), 506-510.
   Virginia Woolf concludes that the biographer is a
craftsman, not an artist, for much of his work is perishable;
but the biographer gives more than facts, for he can give
"the creative fact; the fertile fact; the fact that suggests and
engenders."

WRITING ASSIGNMENTS

1. In "Biography as an Art," James Truslow Adams
says that both Howden Smith in his life of Cornelius Vanderbilt and Gerald W. Johnson in his biography of Andrew
Jackson deal with self-made men., but that their methods
of handling the two men are different. He suggests that
Johnson's fifteenth chapter, "How a Lover Celebrated His
Lady by Saying Nothing," on Rachel Jackson, is a master-
piece and might serve as a model for modern biographers
who "study love in Freud and not in life." Read the two
biographies and write a paper in which you compare the
methods of presentation and styles of these two biographers.

2. Clifford says that the two sources of mistrust of
older editions are the original writers themselves and the
editors. He gives examples of changes that he discovered,
and he tells several stories about how new material was un-
covered mainly by chance. Read two editions of the same
material--letters,. diaries, biographies, notebooks, etc.--one
an early edition and another a recent edition, and compare
the material that you find. Good examples are early editions
and modern scholarly editions of American writers.

3. Randall Stewart found in editing Hawthorne's
American Notebooks and English Notebooks from the original
manuscripts that Mrs. Hawthorne had made many changes,
revisions and omissions, not only in style but also in content, to provide a more favorable picture of her husband.
Select a number of pages from an early edition and compare
these pages with those of a scholarly edition; write a paper
discussing the changes that you have found.

4. Read Ernest Samuels, "Henry Adams and the Gossip Mills," in Essays in American and English Literature. Presented to Bruce Robert McElderry, Jr. Edited by Max F. Schulz, with William D. Templeman and Charles R. Metzger. Athens: Ohio State University Press, 1967, pp. 59-75. Write a paper in which you show how Samuels solved the problem of presenting the gossip of the relationship of Adams and Elizabeth Cameron in his biography of Adams. You may also want to read the sections of the biography that relate to these allegations in Henry Adams: The Middle Years. Cambridge: Harvard University Press.

5. Select an outstanding member of your community or city or someone who has been important in its history and write his biography. You may want to use a member of your family such as your grandfather or grandmother. Consult local documents for your material.

6. Read a biography or an autobiography and write a paper in which you discuss the book from the following standpoints: organization, sources of material, writer's attitude toward his subject, writer's style. Point out examples, if any, where the author uses imaginative detail instead of facts in his narrative. You may use such books as the following:
   (1) Adams, Henry, The Education of Henry Adams, 1906.
   (2) Bowen, Catherine Drinker, Yankee from Olympus, 1944.
   (3) Johnson, James Weldon, Along This Way, 1934.
   (4) Hurston, Zora Neale, Dust Tracks on the Road, 1942.
   (5) Maugham, Somerset, The Summing Up, 1938.
   (6) Sandoz, Marie, Old Jules, 1935.

7. Gorham B. Munson says that prose is the medium favorable to the biographer and the autobiographer because the emotional tension with which we view the courses of our lives or of others' lives is not strong. But there have been autobiographical poems such as Wordsworth's "The Prelude." Read a long autobiographical poem and write a paper presenting the life of the author as revealed in the poem.

8. Read Four Portraits and One Subject: Bernard DeVoto. Boston: Houghton Mifflin Company, 1963. Write a paper in which you combine the four portraits of DeVoto into a composite biography: "The Historian" by Catherine Drinker Bowen, "The Writer" by Edith R. Merrielees, "The Citizen" by Arthur M. Schlesinger, Jr., and "The Personality" by Wallace Stegner.

9. Read "A Memoir" by Robert Fitzgerald in Remembering James Agee, edited by David Madden.   Baton Rouge:
Louisiana State University Press, 1974, pp. 35-94.   Write a
paper in which you discuss the differences in a memoir and
a biography.   Illustrate your statements by referring to Fitzgerald's account.

10.   In The Aspern Papers, Henry James tells the
story of a biographer who will stop at nothing to obtain the
papers of an elderly woman who had once been the lover of
a famous poet.   Read the short novel and write a paper on
the moral nature of biography.

"A lawyer's work requires inordinate amounts of writing which must convey accurate meaning to judges, to other laywers, and to clients. A lawyer who can't write is, quite literally, no lawyer at all."

--Thomas M. Cooley, II, "A Law School Fights Graduate Illiteracy," Saturday Review, XLIV (August 12, 1961), 39.

WRITING IN LAW

Since a lawyer's work requires him to do much writing, a lawyer "who can't write is, quite literally, no lawyer at all." The law student must be able to write clear, exact, and convincing prose. Thus the emphasis in legal writing courses is on organization, development, logical flow. For this reason the composition teacher can teach a course in legal writing without finding it difficult. One writer warns against the use of "heavy-footed jargon" which many lawyers mistake for English. The law student should examine the written opinions of some of the great legal writers as models for his own writing.

1. Brown, John Mason. "Language, Legal and Literary," Saturday Review, XXXV (June 21, 1952), 30-32; (June 28, 1952), 24-26.
In this address before the American Law Institute, May 23, 1952, Brown discusses the similarities between the language of law and the language of literature. He says that law is one of the professions, along with painting, medicine, and music, which may help the writer whether he lives by writing or escapes from it. Chief among the dangers to literature is the "heavy-footed jargon" which so many lawyers mistake for English. "But arguing a case, preparing a brief, or writing a decision offers a superb and muscular exercise in the ordering of facts, the integration of ideas, and the mastery of logic."

2. Cardozo, Benjamin N. "Law and Literature," in The Yale Review Anthology. Edited and with an Introduction by Wilbur Cross and Helen MacAfee. Yale University Press, 1942. Reprinted by Books for Libraries Press, 1971, pp. 183-200.
This article is mainly an exposition of the style of the written decisions of judges. Cardozo says that clearness is the "sovereign virtue" of legal opinions, but that this may be achieved in many ways. "The opinion will need persuasive

force, or the impressive virtue of sincerity and fire, or the
mnemonic power of alliteration and antithesis, or the terse-
ness and tang of the proverb and the maxim. " He discusses
six methods of writing opinions: the type magisterial or im-
perative, which he places first in dignity and power; the type
laconic or sententious; the type conversational or homely; the
type refined or artificial; the type demonstrative or persuasive; and the type tonsorial or agglutinative, which he views
with horror. He also gives some attention to the opinion that
voices a dissent, to the element of humor in judicial opinions,
and to the writing of arguments of the bar. Cardozo concludes that cases are made great not by something intrinsic
in the cases but in what the judge or advocate makes of them.
"He [the judge or advocate] is expounding a science, or a
body of truth which he seeks to assimilate to a science, but
in the process of exposition, he is practicing an art. "

     3. Cooley, Thomas M. , II. "A Law School Fights
Graduate Illiteracy, " Saturday Review, XLIV (August 12,
1961), 39-41.
     Cooley, Dean of the School of Law of the University
of Pittsburgh, complains about the inability of beginning students at his law school to write clear and acceptable English.
Since a lawyer's work requires much writing that must convey accurate meaning to clients, to other lawyers, and to
judges, Cooley says that a lawyer "who can't write is, quite
literally, no lawyer at all. " Since he believes that the only
way to learn to write is by writing, the School of Law, University of Pittsburgh, requires the writing of legal papers in
each of the three years, beginning with the task of composing
a brief or précis of an actual legal opinion and continuing
with other papers related to the law courses being pursued.
It was found that students who do large amounts of legal writing as members of the staff which edits the law review of
the school obtain a training superior to those who do not.
This superiority was accompanied by a grasp of legal thought
"which goes far beyond the content of the materials with which
law review students work. There is something almost mys-
tical in the process. "

     4. Crystal, David, and Derek Davy. "The Language
of Legal Documents, " in Investigating English Style. Bloom-
ington: Indiana University Press, 1969, pp. 193-215.
     This practical analysis of the language of legal docu-
ments includes a discussion of how sentence structure, clause
structure, punctuation, modification, noun and verb groups,
and vocabulary may be manipulated to produce precision of

meaning. Legal language may vary according to the purpose of the document, but changes come slowly. Legal writing is also limited in that it must "always behave in conformity with the body of rules--the law of which it is the vehicle. Certain things must be said in certain ways for fear of seeming to misrepresent the law, and before they may be said differently the law itself must often consent."

5. Highet, Gilbert. "The Prose of the Law," in Explorations. New York: Oxford University Press, 1971, pp. 334-350.

Although this article is mainly a review of an anthology of the prose of law, Voices in Court: A Treasury of the Bench, the Bar, and the Courtroom, compiled by W. H. Davenport, 1958, Highet discusses the value to lawyers of an understanding of language and of the ability to write clear, exact, and convincing prose, for, he says, "lawyers depend on language: they write it, read it, analyze it, line by line."

6. Howe, Laurence Lee. "Historical Method and Legal Education," American Association of University Professors Bulletin, XXXVI (1950), 346-356.

Howe says that since history is a method of investigation as well as a method of describing and interpreting the results of investigation, training in historical research is of value as a part of the pre-professional training of the law student. He describes the method used in the preparation of historical monographs--isolation of the problem, the research, and the conclusion--and says that this training is good training for the pre-law student. "The only essential part of pre-law education is the teaching of the ability to evaluate written and spoken evidence, to discover the truth, and to present the results of one's investigation, in writing and in speaking, in a clear and convincing manner. . . . But no lawyer can possibly succeed without learning to think, write, and speak clearly."

7. "The Language of Law, a Symposium," Western Law Review, IX (March, 1958), 117-198.

In addition to a "Preface" by Walter Probert, symposium editor, and a "Foreword" by Justice V. Schaefer, there are five articles which concern the relation of language to the judicial process: "Practicing Law and General Semantics" by Edward B. Duffy; "Law, Logic and Communication" by Walter Probert; "Facts, Evidence and Legal Proof" by Lee Loevinger; "Semantics, Law and 'Priestly-Minded Men'" by S. I. Hayakawa; and "The Value Analysis of Legal Discourse" by Harold D. Lasswell.

8. Levitan, Mortimer. "Dissertation on Writing Legal Opinion," Wisconsin Law Review, (January, 1960), 22-38.
A quasi-serious discussion of the "garden variety of legal opinions requested by government agencies and commercial concerns."

9. Melinkoff, David. The Language of the Law. Boston: Little, Brown and Company, 1963. 526 pp.
The purpose of this book, written by a member of the California bar, is to discuss ways to make the language of the law rational and practical. It is organized into three parts: Part One, "What Is the Language of the Law?"; Part Two, "History of the Language of the Law"; and Part Three, "Using the Language of the Law." There are also a "Selected Bibliography" and a "Word and Phrase Index."

10. White, John O., and Norman Brand. "Composition for the Pre-Professional: Focus on Legal Writing," College Composition and Communication, XXVII (February, 1976), 41-46.
Since most of the writing of a lawyer is intended to clarify, the pre-law student should be taught to write so that the ordinary reader will understand the issue, the reasoning, and the conclusion of any paper. The law student is expected to write legal memoranda and briefs in which he argues a certain position. He will also have to write a law examination. Since the emphasis in legal writing is on organization, development, logical flow, and clarity, the composition teacher can teach such a course without finding it difficult. The authors warn the instructor to be aware of the students' attempts to write the way they think lawyers write and to be alert to inflated language in all of its forms.

WRITING ASSIGNMENT

1. Read John Adams's "Speech in Defense of the Soldiers," in The Colonial Idiom, edited by David Potter and Gordon L. Thomas. Carbondale, Ill.: Southern Illinois University Press, 1970, pp. 108-132, and write a paper in which you present Adams's arguments.

CHAPTER 4

WRITING IN SCIENCE

"Great writing in science must come from inside the discipline, and everything will depend on the rare talent which can break through the meshes of technical vocabulary to express itself in words of common usage."

--Barbara W. Tuchman, "The Historian's Opportunity," Saturday Review, L (January-March, 1967), 130-131.

"The aim of science is to discover and illuminate truth. And that, I take it, is the aim of literature, whether biography or history or fiction; it seems to me, then there can be no separate literature of science."

--Rachel Carson, "National Book Award Acceptance Speech," in Paul Brooks, The House of Life. Rachel Carson at Work. Boston: Houghton Mifflin Company, 1972, p. 128.

WRITING IN SCIENCE

Scientific writing should be simple, clear, accurate, and a pleasure for the ordinary person to read, for it is the function of the science writer to inform. The writer should be familiar with the subject matter and he should keep in mind his audience, his purpose, and the structure of his material. Several of the writers in this section say that writing helps the student to think more clearly and to read more attentively. One writer suggests that reading good writers will cause the student to absorb the style of the writer.

1. Baker, John R. "English Style in Scientific Papers," Science, CXXIII (April, 1956), 713-714. Reprinted from Nature, CLXXVI (1955).
The purpose of this article is to suggest ways by which scientific papers in British scientific journals may be made simpler, clearer, and more pleasant to read. Baker says that the faults in passages in scientific papers that are least in accord with good English style are in grammar, grandiloquence, and German construction. Of the first, he mentions particularly the use of present participles and gerunds; of the second, the use of Latin phrases, long words derived from Greek or Latin roots, elaborate ways of expression, the use of abstract words, "genteelism" and archaic words, vogue-words, especially negative vogue-words; of the third, the piling-up before a noun of words that are not adjectives but are used adjectively, a process familiar to the German language. To improve scientific writing, Baker makes the following suggestions: examine standard handbooks and books on writing; teach students to correct errors found in scientific papers; read good writing to absorb the style of the writer.

2. Barber, C. L. "Some Measurable Characteristics of Modern Scientific Prose," Contributions to English Syntax

and Philology.   Gothenburg Studies in English.   Edited by
Frank Behre, XIV (1962), 21-43.
    A study of the characteristics of modern scientific
prose based on excerpts from three different texts used in
university teaching of science with overseas students.   Text
A is a selection from a book on the engineering applications
of electronics.   Text B is concerned with basic research in
biochemistry.   Text C, from an elementary university textbook
on astronomy, consists of a chapter on astronomical instruments.   Each of these texts includes two scientific fields:
electronics and engineering, biology and chemistry, astronomy
and instrumental optics.   Barber compares some of his findings with those of three of his colleagues: one from the
University of Leeds, one from Poland, and one from West
Pakistan.   Barber's analysis consists of a study of sentence
structure, verb forms, and vocabulary.   He examines sentence length, clause types, verb tenses, and the use of non-
finite verbs.   Detailed analyses of these items are included
in the study.

    3. Burkett, David Warren. Writing Science News for
the Mass Media.   Houston, Texas: Gulf Publishing Company,
1965.   183 pp.
    A practical guide for those interested in writing
science news stories for a non-scientific audience.   Begun
as a master's thesis for the University of Texas School of
Journalism, it covers such topics as the function of the
science writer, the elements of science news, the ways science writers gather material, the expanding fields of science
writing, ethics in science writing, science and censorship.
A reference list of fifteen pages is included.

    4. Carson, Rachel. "National Book Award Acceptance
Speech," in The House of Life.   Rachel Carson at Work, by
Paul Brooks.   Boston: Houghton Mifflin Company, 1972, pp.
127-219.
    In this short acceptance speech for the National Book
Award for The Sea Around Us, Carson says her purpose in
the book was to portray the subject of the sea profile with
"fidelity and understanding," for the aim of science, as the
aim of literature, is "to discover and illuminate truth."
Thus there can be no separate literature of science.   She
says that the sea had been part of her own life from her
earliest childhood and that she had written only what she
thought and felt about it.

    5. Gilman, William. "The Bad Language of Science,"
South Atlantic Quarterly, LVIII (Autumn, 1959), 556-567.

Gilman says that communication between technicians and the ordinary person is bogged down with jargon and with illiterate and careless handling of the language. Even when the average technician uses words that are understandable in themselves, the statements are often ambiguous. He says there is a need for authors who are familiar with the special language of technology and with the ways to solve practical writing problems. Clarity, he says, is essential to technical writing, and clarity requires a knowledge of facts, honesty, and the ability to choose the right word. He says that applied science is turning to special courses in writing and to workshops for technical editors. He thinks the difficulties would not be so great if the trend toward specialization were reversed to broader fields of learning. The embryo technicians cannot write because they cannot read.

6. Gilman, William. The Language of Science. A Guide to Effective Writing. New York: Harcourt, Brace and World, Inc., 1961. 248 pp.

A discussion about writing designed to assist scientists and engineers to explain science and technology not only to each other but also to the public at large. It deals with such topics as how to interest the reader, how to say what one means, how to achieve clarity, and how to write with style. At the end of the first chapter, Gilman offers five guiding principles to improve writing: read well-written prose--its "how-to" will become a part of your writing; take time to re-write, for it straightens your thinking; bend rigid rules to suit your purpose; do not forget the reader; when in doubt, use common sense.

7. Kellogg, Charles E. "What Makes Good Scientific Writing," in The Wonderful World of Books. Edited by Alfred Steffernd. Boston: Houghton Mifflin Company, 1953, pp. 194-198.

Kellogg says there is a need for good scientific and technical books and that these books should be well written. He lists the requirements for good scientific writing: it must be accurate; it must be clear; it should avoid vague general terms. He offers two main rules for the scientific writer: have clearly in mind what you want to say and say it as simply as possible and still be clear and accurate. The scientific writer should decide on his audience and write for the convenience of his audience. He should be a specialist in information about his subject, but he should have a broad point of view, developed by experience and reading; he should be enthusiastic about his subject but not to the point of exaggeration. The writing should be both reliable and reasonable. Four questions should be raised about the author of a scientific or technical book: Has he followed the scientific method honestly and competently? Is he free to tell the truth as he sees it? Has his work been tested through free and open criticism by scholars in the same field? Has he the respect of competent colleagues in his field?

8. Rapaport, Anatol. "The Language of Science: Its Simplicity, Beauty, and Humor," ETC: A Review of General Semantics, XVI (Summer, 1959), 445-458.
Rapaport argues that in the areas of science where the richest and most profound insights abound, mainly in mathematics and physics, the vocabularies consist of short, commonly-used words and the elements of poetry abound. But the language of science uses very simple words to denote exceedingly complex notions. "Science has freed the intellect from dependence on concrete visualizable conceptualization-- largely through introducing mathematical operation as a generator of concepts. It is this semantic device which makes a comparatively small vocabulary sufficient for physics.'

9. Savory, Theodore H. The Language of Science. London: Andre Deutsch, Limited. Revised Edition, 1967. 173 pp.
Savory presents a discussion of the words of scientific language and the growth of thisl language as well as the nature of scientific prose. The last two chapters are concerned with scientists and their writings and with outstanding books on the literature of science.

10. Science and Language. Selected Essays. Edited by Alfred M. Bork. Boston: D. C. Heath and Company, 1966. 113 pp. (Paper)
A collection of nine essays chosen to help students to "explore the ways in which our verbal assumptions can affect scientific work, or the ways in which scientific arguments may be mustered in the arena of verbal persuasion; they do not deal concretely with the problems of expressing scientific knowledge in language structures." The essays were chosen for their intrinsic interest, but not according to any special thesis. They range in time from the Victorian period to the present.

11. Scientists as Writers. Edited by J. Harrison. Cambridge, Mass.: Massachusetts Institute of Technology, 1965. 206 pp. (Paper)

A collection of prose passages by scientists about
science arranged according to eleven themes: Nature of the
Universe; Nature of Matter; Nature of Life; Nature of Mind;
Nature of Science; Likenesses; Cause and Effect or Blind
Chance?; Evolution and Man; Our Own Worst Enemies; Science
and Art; Science and Religion. Although most of the selections are from modern authors, some of them go back as far
as Aristotle. Notes supplement each selection.

12. Woodbury, David. "Writing about Science," in
Writers on Writing. Edited by Herschel Brickell. New
York: Doubleday and Company, Inc., 1949, pp. 167-179.
To become a writer on scientific subjects, Woodbury
says that one must have the right attitude toward science;
that is, one must respect science and must apply understanding, appreciation, and humility in his reporting. The
writer must keep in mind his audience, his purpose, and
the structure of his material. His writing must have human
interest through the use of living people in the narrative.
To know where you are going in your writing requires a
thorough knowledge of material. Closely related are clarity
of statement and effective style. He gives hints for an
actual job of writing: For material, stay fairly close to
your own field, select a subject that is of news interest, get
more information than you will need through reading and interviewing. Rewrite and expand your notes and plan your
paper. Make only a simple outline that can be changed as
you write. After writing, check and recheck for facts and
for effect. Rewrite and cut if necessary. Regard your
work "with seriousness, with dignity, and with humility."

13. Woodford, F. Peter. "Sounder Thinking Through
Clearer Writing," Science, CLVI, No. 3776 (May 12, 1967),
743-745.
Woodford objects to the poor writing found in scholarly
journals, not only because it often conveys a meaning not intended but because it exerts a corrupting influence on the
writing, reading, and thinking of young scientists. He provides illustrations of this corruption from the writing and
reading of his own students. But he has also found positive
results in the course of teaching scientific writing. "The
most striking observation is that by teaching writing you can
actually strengthen students' ability not only to write but
also to read more attentively and to think more logically and
rigorously." The discipline required in putting words into
formal sentences and in writing them down and examining the
statements helps to clarify thinking. Woodford would like to

have writing as a regular part of scientific thinking, for the
object of university training, he says, is not so much the
acquisition of knowledge as the development of the power to
think.

WRITING ASSIGNMENTS

1. Make a study of a folk medicine or remedy that
has been used by country people over the years and write a
paper in which you try to determine its scientific basis, if
any. Some of the ideas you may want to investigate: the
use of the madstone for preventing hydrophobia and for curing
snake or insect bites; the wearing of garlic or drugs around
the neck to prevent certain diseases. Or, you may study the
problem of planting crops according to the moon, or the use
of a well witch for discovering water. You may want to
read Emily and Per Ola d' Autaire, "The Forked-Stick Phe-
nomenon," Saturday Evening Post, May/June, 1976, pp. 32-
35, 85, and The Beginner's Handbook of Dowsing, Crown
Publishers, before you begin work on water-witching.

2. Locate two articles, one written in purely scientific language and one written in literary style, and compare
the differences in the way the two articles are written.
Good examples of the second group are The Immense Journey
by Loren Eiseley, 1946; The Desert Year by Joseph Wood
Krutch, 1951; The Mountains of California by John Muir,
1894; Piñon Country by Haniel Long, 1941; The Edge of the
Sea by Rachel Carson, 1955.

3. Lewis Thomas has written an interesting article
about the sounds that animals and insects make to each other
in "Notes of a Biology Watcher," Harper's Magazine, February, 1973, pp. 98-99. Read this article and then make a
study of your own observations of how animals or insects
that you know communicate.

4. In "Synchronous Fireflies," Scientific American,
CCXXXIV (May, 1976), 74-85, John and Elizabeth Buck write
that the flashing of fireflies in the temperate zones is un-
synchronized, while certain species of Asia and the Pacific
flash in unison. Read this article and others listed below
and write a paper in which you present explanations for the
differences in their behavior. Additional articles: John and
Elizabeth Buck, "Mechanism of Rhythmic Synchronous Flashing
of Fireflies," Science, CLIX, No. 3821 (March 22, 1968),

1319-1327; John Bonner Buck, "Synchronous Rhythmic Flashing of Fireflies," The Quarterly Review of Biology, XIII, No. 3 (September, 1938), 301-314; J. E. Lloyd, "Model for the Mating Protocol of Synchronously Flashing Fireflies," Nature, CCXXXXV, No. 5423 (October 5, 1973), 268-270.

5. Write a paper in which you give scientific explanation of the celestial navigation of birds. You may need to do some reading before you begin.

CHAPTER 5

TECHNICAL AND BUSINESS WRITING

"In my opinion," says Professor Edward Kilduff of New York University's School of Commerce, "the most effective kind of English composition being taught today ... is the realistic, practical non-literary American type that we find in such courses as business writing, engineering writing, newspaper writing, publicity writing, and advertising writing."

--Quoted in "The Language of Business," Fortune, XLII (November, 1950), 140.

TECHNICAL AND BUSINESS WRITING

Technical writing is an important field if technology is to have its proper influence on the social problems of today. The technical writer has a duty not only to his fellow technicians but to the ordinary reader to write in a clear and logical manner so that the reader gets the exact meaning of the writer. Ideas as to the kind of technical writing courses vary, but many of the writers included in this section agree that college English courses as they now stand do not provide the necessary training for technical writers since they adhere almost exclusively to the study of and the writing about literature. One writer says that good writing is grounded in a liberal arts education. He suggests that technical readings be included in such courses as English, foreign languages, and philosophy to bridge the gap between the humanities and technology courses. Although clear and forceful writing is an important part of business transactions, it is apt to receive little formal and intelligent attention from the management. When an individual in business desires to improve his writing, his company owes him sensible and concrete advice.

1. Boltwood, Robert M. "Technical Writing--And English," College Composition and Communication, XI (December, 1960), 226-228.
A report of the discussion by five panelists of industrial writers for the January 1960 seminar of the Southeastern Michigan Chapter, Society of Technical Writers and Publishers. The panelists agree that the technical writer provides practical information, that his style is objective exposition, and that he must know his subject as well as the background of his readers. They mention that college English courses had played a minor role in the backgrounds of technical writers, but that they had learned from other courses: basic speech, law, chemistry, mathematics, physics, and biology. One writer mentions his training in logic.

2. Britton, W. Earl. "What Is Technical Writing?" College Composition and Communication, XVI (May, 1965), 113-116.

Britton gives the definitions and approaches to technical writing as seen by several writers on the subject and concludes with his own definition. He thinks that the primary characteristic of technical and scientific writing lies in the effort of the writer to convey only one meaning in what he says. Such writing allows no interpretation by the reader except that intended by the writer. But this does not require the style to be "flat and drab."

3. Ewing, David W. Writing for Results: In Business, Government, and the Professions. New York: John Wiley and Sons, Inc., 1974. 466 pp.

Aimed at helping readers to acquire writing skills useful in their future professional activities, the book is divided into three sections: a short background section presenting an overview and philosophy intended to help the business writer make decisions about purpose and objectives; practical advice on strategies and organization; methods of achieving suitable tone and style, as well as tips on matters of coherence and grammatical correctness. Case problems at the end of each chapter provide practice. Examples of how best to handle "muddy paragraphs," and advice on the use of tables and charts are also included.

4. Fielden, John. "'What do you mean I can't write?'" Harvard Business Review, XLII (March, 1964), 144-156.

Fielden says that complaints about students' inability to write should be narrowed to specific items. He considers writing for business under four basic categories: readability, correctness, appropriateness, and thought. By readability he means a clear style of writing which he says is dependent on the reader's background for understanding the material, the sentence structure, proper paragraph construction, clear transitions between paragraphs, simplicity of language, and the ability of the writer to prepare the reader by stating the purpose and the direction of the paper at the beginning. The final aspect of readability Fielden identifies as "focus," the directing of the reader's attention to the important points. Correctness, says Fielden, is not confined to grammar and punctuation but is more closely related to coherence, the placing of related words, sentences, and paragraphs so that the writing is read clearly and with ease. Fielden divides appropriateness into two main types: the type that a superior writes to his subordinate and the type that the subordinate writes to his superior. In the first, he includes facts, supporting detail, and attitude. For the second type, "straight talk, carefully and tactfully couched, is the only sensible policy." Aspects of thought include the intellectual competence of the writer, fidelity to the assignment, and the ability to draw conclusions.

5. Freedman, Morris. "The Seven Sins of Technical Writing," College Composition and Communication, IX (February, 1958), 10-16.
    Freedman says that technical writing must be judged by standards higher than that for other writing since technical writing is functional and errors could lead to disastrous results. Freedman discusses what he lists as the seven cardinal sins of technical writing: the writer's indifference to the reader--writing down or elaborating the obvious; fuzziness--vague words, meaningless words, or wrong words; emptiness--use of jargon and big words, pretentious words where normal words are available; wordiness; bad habits-- pat phrases, awkward expressions, confusing sentence structure; the deadening passive; mechanical errors. Technical writing, Freedman insists, "should be as clean, as functional, as inevitable as any modern machine designed to do a job well."

6. Freedman, Morris. "Technical Writing Anyone?" College Composition and Communication, X (February, 1959), 53-57.
    Freedman says that good writing must be grounded in a liberal arts education and that technical writers without such a background confuse writing with having a large vocabulary and a knowledge of grammar and punctuation. Such writers think of technical writing as being on the same level as the skill of a stenographer. Freedman places the blame on both the schools of technology and the English departments who fail to require students to read such writers as Hume, Huxley, and Russell. Engineering students in many universities are either excused from courses in literature, or are subjected to quick surveys in humanities courses. Freedman says that the ideal technical writer should be basically trained in the humanities, especially in English, with additional preparation in foreign languages, as well as his training in technology. He suggests that a bridge to technology and science be given the humanities student by introducing him to such magazines as Scientific American in English classes, to technical selections in French and German in introductory

language courses, and to a mathematical journal in philosophy classes.

    7. Handbook of Technical Writing Practices. Edited by Stella Jordan and Associate Editors Joseph M. Kleenman and H. Lee Shimberg. New York: Wiley-Interscience, 1971. Volumes I and II. 1374 pp.

    Published in cooperation with the Society for Technical Communication, this two-volume handbook covers the main practices of technical writing used by both military and commercial concerns. Volume I (Part I) is concerned with the documents and publications written and produced by technical writers. Volume II (Parts II, III, IV) is concerned with illustrating, editing, data-processing; the management of technical writing; guides and references used in technical writing. Each of the thirty-two chapters is written by an authority in the field.

    8. "The Language of Business," Fortune, XLII (November, 1950), 113-117, 134, 136, 138, 140.

    The author of this article says that business has become almost as extensive a publisher as the government itself. A large amount of the language of business has become incomprehensible to the people it is trying to reach, and it is enormously expensive in time and money. The written variety, impersonal and filled with jargon, is known as businesese. The spoken variety is found at banquet tables, at conventions, and at conferences. This might be called reverse gobbledegook. It is "English that is on the beam. English with its feet on the ground, in short, shirt-sleeve English." Some businesses have set up programs to improve business English. There is also the "plain talk" movement, a sort of prose-engineering program, for its core is the use of techniques to achieve readability. It advocates a decrease in the use of jargon and it is enthusiastic about the use of colloquial speech. But talking and writing are not the same thing, and such a belief encourages sloppiness and faulty thinking. Simplicity is not dependent on short words and short sentences but on discipline and organization of thought. The writer says that this whole prose-engineering movement is a measure of the growing specialization in our society as well as of the failure of our schools and colleges. We do not need more "applied" English courses, but we do need better basic ones.

    9. Massirer, Mary. "'Nuts-and-Bolts' English: The Technical Writing Course," Proceedings of the Conference of

College Teachers of English of Texas, XXXVIII (September, 1973), 43-47.
A course in technical writing allows the student to become familiar with practical writing procedures and to learn how writing fits into the total pattern of his professional activity. He must learn the conventions of good writing, the language used by scientists, and the use of graphic aids such as tables, graphs, and charts. His writing culminates in a formal report, a project which teaches him how to gather material in addition to library reading, and how to prepare the final form of the report--the title page and abstract, the table of contents, a list of tables and illustrations, conclusions and recommendations, bibliography, appendix, and index.

10. Mills, Gordon H., and John A. Walter. Technical Writing. New York: Holt, Rinehart and Winston, Inc. Third Edition, 1970. 573 pp.
Designed to bridge the gap between professional writing of scientists and engineers and a course for students of technical writing, this book is divided into six main sections and an appendix of seven parts. Section One is concerned with a general discussion of technical writing, its basic principles, style in technical writing, outlines and abstracts. Section Two discusses special techniques of technical writing. Section Three has to do with transitions, introductions, and conclusions. Section Four analyzes types of reports. Section Five discusses report layout. Section Six is concerned with the Library Research Report.

11. Pearsall, Thomas E. "Introduction: Audience Analysis," in Audience Analysis for Technical Writing. Beverly Hills, Calif.: Glencoe Press, 1969, pp. ix-xxii.
Pearsall divides the audiences for technical writing into five groups: the layman, the executive, the expert, the technician, and the operator, but he explains that no group is homogeneous and that his own statements are generalizations. The writer must analyze his own audience and provide information and write in language suitable to the group. Pearsall stresses the use of simple language and illustrations for the layman, information about people and profits for the executive, facts for the expert, practical and specific instructions for the technician, simple directions for the operator with generous use of visual aids.

12. Salant, Walter S. "Miscellany--Writing and Reading in Economics," Journal of Political Economy, LXVII (July/August, 1969), 545-558.

Salant criticizes the writing of professional economists, their "obscure and clumsy writing," resulting from "poor thinking or a feeble grasp of the principles of clear expression." He stresses the importance of using exact words and of preventing confusion by the use of proper punctuation, clear pronoun antecedents, and avoiding the use of clichés and dangling participles. He also warns economists not to use mathematical notation in expository writing unless the verbal statement would be more complicated for the reader. He urges the writer to strive not only for clarity but also for "conciseness, force, and even vividness" since these elements help the reader to retain his interest in the writing.

13. Sawyer, Thomas M. "Rhetoric in an Age of Science and Technology," College Composition and Communication, XXIII (December, 1972), 390-398.
Sawyer says that the demand for people trained in the kind of rhetoric employed by the graduates in science and technology is likely to increase since these people do a lot of writing, especially of articles and abstracts. The present program of freshman composition has little value for those students who major in scientific and technological disciplines since it is concerned mainly with literature.

14. Souther, J. W. "The Expanding Dimension of Technical Writing," College Composition and Communication, XXII (May, 1971), 185-187.
Since scientific and technical writing is important in relating technology to social problems, Souther says there is a need for colleges to expand their technical writing programs. He reports on a proposed Master's program in Medical and Technical Communication which is to prepare its graduates to work in four areas: as science writers or editors for newspapers, magazines, television, etc.; as writers and editors on the staffs of professional periodicals, commercial publishers of professional books, and of university presses; as writers, editors, and publications managers in government, industry, public health, and higher education; as teachers of technical communication in undergraduate programs. Souther lists the principles and knowledge that the program is designed to develop as well as the courses already on campus that can contribute to the technical writing program. In addition, he discusses the opportunities for practical experience in writing and editing to be found on the campus, especially in writing and editing papers, books, periodicals, TV programs, etc.

15. The Teaching of Technical Writing. Edited by
Donald H. Cunningham and Herman A. Estrin. Urbana,
Ill.: National Council of Teachers of English, 1975. 221
pp. (Paper)
A collection of twenty-four articles designed to help
teachers of English who are responsible for teaching courses
in technical and scientific writing. These articles are grouped
in eight sections: Technical Writing Defined; Teaching Tech-
nical Writing; Skills, Needs, and Goals of the Technical
Writing Student; Technical Writing Teachers Appraise the
Curriculum; Technical Writing in Action; Evaluating Technical
Writing; The Nexus; School and Industry; Technical Writing:
The Science and the Art.

16. Waldo, W. H. "Teaching Report Writing to Professional Chemists and Chemical Engineers," Journal of
Chemical Education, XXXIII, No. 2 (February, 1956), 59-61.
A summary of a report based on 110 replies to a
questionnaire sent to industrial and governmental members
of the Chemical Literature Division concerning on-the-job
training courses to teach chemists and chemical engineers to
write better. The report concerns the selection of teachers,
the size of classes, the types of subject matter taught in the
courses, the preparation of graphic material, clarity and
organization in papers, and student reactions to the course.
Waldo concludes that the success of a formal report writing
training course "lies in the teacher's knowledge of the students' needs and his care in tailor-making his presentation to
meet them."

17. Yale, Stanley L. "Writing Courses for Engineers,"
Improving College and University Teaching, XIX (Winter,
1971), 60-61.
Yale says that the engineer needs to have writing competence, for poorly written articles are an expense to industry,
a bore for the reader, and a damage to the reputation of the
engineer. Many of the modern engineering schools have added
courses in technical writing. Yale describes a required
course for seniors in the Engineering Department of Newark
College of Engineering known as "Engineering Report Writing."
This course uses technical professional magazines, a text on
technical writing, and a book of readings to supplement the
class discussions. The student begins by writing an abstract
of a technical article and an analysis of an article from a
professional magazine. After the student has learned to distinguish between good and bad writing, he makes a detailed
study of a professional magazine. Other written work is done

in class, but all work is expected to be correct in spelling, punctuation, sentence structure, and grammar. Near the end of the course a formal report is prepared and submitted to the instructor of another course in the Civil Engineering Department. The subject is chosen by the student but it must relate to the other course. The final assignment is a paper on the style of technical writing.

(A report on this course is given in H. A. Estrin, "An Engineering Writing Course," Classroom Practices in the Teaching of English. Edited by A. J. Beeler. Urbana, Illinois: National Council of the Teachers of English, 1966, pp. 79-83, and in The Teaching of Technical Writing, pp. 102-106.)

WRITING ASSIGNMENTS

1. Read "The Composite Business Speech" in Fortune, XLII (November, 1950), 114, and write a paper in which you analyze it as a sample of the usual business language. You may want to compare it with some of Babbitt's speeches in Sinclair Lewis's Babbitt.

2. Make a collection of at least five business reports that you locate in magazines or from businesses you know and make a study of their content, organization, and language. Or, you may make the same kind of study of business letters of various kinds: letters of application, complaint, of advertising, etc.

CHAPTER 6

INTERDISCIPLINARY WRITING

Literature and Other Disciplines
  Literature and Language
  Literature and History
  Literature and Biography
  Literature and Law
  Literature and Science
  Literature, History, and Science

History and Other Disciplines
  History and Biography
  History and Science

Language and Politics

"Between thought and style there is a constant and necessary interaction. Turgid thought cannot flow in crystal-clear language; a slovenly mind is not capable of a careful selection of words, so as to give to each word its full value and right connotations, and to each idea its exact and fitting expression; and to be truly discreet though vocal, free though not silent, requires skill in the use of language. In turn, constant, diligent care of language and style is a mental discipline; it pays to undergo it. Bad writing is like bad cooking--it corrupts and wastes good material, and in the long run is apt to affect the digestion. Cruelty to food can hardly be eradicated in this country; but cruelty to English can be prevented."

--L. B. Namier, "English Prose," in Conflicts: Studies in Contemporary History. London, 1942. Reprinted by Books for Libraries Press, 1969, p. 218.

"If it be said that politics has nothing to do with literature, or that the form of a document can be appreciated without reference to its content, I do not agree. On the contrary, it is a favorite notion of mine that in literary discourse form and content are two aspects of the same thing."

--Carl Becker, The Declaration of Independence. Second Edition. New York: Alfred A. Knopf, 1942, p. xiii.

LITERATURE AND OTHER DISCIPLINES

LITERATURE AND LANGUAGE

Language is the medium of literature and it is inseparable from the thought and the effect produced. The metalinguists go even further and say that language is not only the
means of presenting ideas but may be the shaper of thought
itself. The interplay of language and literary art is shown
in the writer's choice of words, in the sentence structure, in
language used to define character, in the rhythm and imagery
of poetry, and in the emotional effect of the total combination.

1. Chase, Stuart. "How Language Shapes Our
Thoughts, " Harper's Magazine, CCVI (April, 1954), 76-82.
Chase says that the structure of the language we use
affects our thought and may even be prior to thought. He
discusses the work of the metalinguists, especially the work
of Benjamin Lee Whorf, who demonstrate that the forms of
a person's thoughts are controlled by patterns learned early
and that language is not a tool but a shaper of thought itself.
The structure of each language, says Whorf, "is not merely
a reproducing instrument for voicing ideas but rather is itself the shaper of ideas, the program and guide for the individual's mental activity." Whorf also says that the world is
presented to us in a flux of impressions which have to be
organized by the linguistic system built into our minds.

2. Ciardi, John. "The Act of Language, " in Adventures of the Mind. Second Series. Edited by Richard
Thruelsen and John Kobler. New York: Vintage Books,
1959, 1960, 1961, pp. 307-324.
Ciardi says that to read a poem with no thought in
mind but to paraphrase it in a prose statement is the destruction of poetry. The poet must be passionate about the
four elements of poetry--rhythm, diction, image, and form--

for these are the life of a poem. The meaning of the poem
is not in the subject, says Ciardi, but in the way the poetic
involvement transfigures the subject, that is, in the act of
language. Good poetry will fasten itself in human memory
because man is the language animal and his "need of language is from the roots of his consciousness." But nothing
in a good poem happens by accident. The poet finds joy in
the form and management of the poem, and the reader
learns imagination, precision, and correspondence from the
poet. "The act of the poem is in its act of language."

     3. Costello, Donald P. "The Language of The
Catcher in the Rye," American Speech, XXXIV (October,
1959), 172-181.
     Costello says that a study of the language in The
Catcher in the Rye can be justified not only for its literary
interest but for its linguistic significance. He says that
Salinger had the problem of creating an individual character
who would speak in a language typical of teenagers in general.
The two major speech habits that he gives to Holden are his
use of ending his thoughts with a loosely dangling "and all,"
and the insistent "I really did." Closely allied is Holden's
habit of insisting "if you want to know the truth." Costello
also mentions Holden's use of crude and vulgar language, his
use of slang, his repetitious and trite vocabulary, his habit
of turning nouns into adjectives and of using nouns as adverbs, and his violation of rules of grammar. Costello concludes that the language of The Catcher in the Rye is an
"authentic artistic rendering of a type of informal, colloquial,
teenage American spoken speech."

     4. Creswell, Thomas J. "Literary Dialect in Nelson
Algren's 'Never Come Morning,'" in Studies in Linguistics in
Honor of Raven I. McDavid, Jr. Edited by Lawrence N.
Davis. University of Alabama Press, 1972, pp. 29-40.
     In his novel Never Come Morning, Algren's charac-
ters are almost exclusively Polish-American. The methods
he uses to indicate this are of several kinds. Surnames and
in some cases their given names and nicknames indicate
their national origin. In moments of extreme stress some
of the characters lapse into their native language. To indicate first-generation characters, Algren regularly uses the
omission of pronomial subject, of future tense markers, and
of conjunctions. Other characteristics of the language include the omission of the article a, of the expletic it, of that
in a series, of the infinitive sign to; the failure to inflect the
verb, the substitution of for for to and for for of, the use of

appended second person vocative, and of misplaced adverbs.
There are a few indications of variations in pronunciation
and only a trifling use of Polish proverbs.

5.   Daiches, David.   "The Literary Use of Language,"
in A Study of Literature for Readers and Critics.   New York:
W. W. Norton and Company, Inc.   Norton Library Edition,
1948, pp. 21-46.
    Daiches says that language can be regarded as a
means of communication, or, in addition to communicating,
of expanding the significance of the communication.   This
last use is the literary use of language.   The difference in
the two is in the difference in the degree of control exer-
cised by the writer.

6.   Halle, Louis J.   "The Language of Statesmen,"
Saturday Review, LIV (October 16, 1971), 30-31.
    Halle uses Lincoln's Gettysburg Address and his
Second Inaugural Address as examples of language that is
poetry, but he says that the address of Secretary of State
George Marshall, February 22, 1947, in which he appealed
to the American people to accept their world responsibility,
was written "in language that would hardly have served for
an argument in favor of raising the postman's salary."
Halle thinks that it is the function of political leaders to
enshrine our visions of a noble life in the forms of language
as the painters, sculptors, and musicians enshrine them in
the graphic arts.   "At the highest level, then, as perhaps
at the lowest, too, thought and language are inseparable."

7.   Morris, J. Allen.   "Gullah in the Stories and
Novels of William Gilmore Simms," American Speech, XXII
(1947), 46-53.
    Morris says that the character of Negro Tom in
Simms's story "A Scene of the Revolution" (1833) is probably
the first Negro character to speak accurate Gullah in an
American short story.   Simms wrote four other stories and
at least nine novels in which Negroes are employed as characters.   Morris compares Simms's Gullah dialect with that
used later by Ambrose E. Gonzales and finds the dialects
very similar.   He says that Simms's use of the dialect fits
smoothly into the framework of the laws and analogies of
Gullah worked out by Dr. Reed Smith.   Morris recommends
Simms's story "The Lazy Crow" as an interesting story that
provides a good example of Simms's use of Gullah.

8.   Seary, E. R., and G. M. Story.   "Literature and

Language, " in Study of English, A Handbook for Students. New York: St. Martin's Press, 1962, pp. 13-21.

English literature, especially the poetry, is shaped by the nature of the language. English poetry is governed by the native stress patterns of the language, and it is essential that it be read aloud, for the sound is often as important as the sense. The sentence structure of English also shows the dependence of literature on language. Style is largely the result of the individual writer's variation of the basic sentence patterns of the language. The interplay of language and art is also shown in a writer's choice of words, for English is a combination of simple, native words and words of foreign derivations. Some older writers require the reader to know something of the language at its various historical periods. The attention of the relation of language to literature is useful in that it encourages the accurate study of the meaning of a work as well as a close reading of the text. It also serves as a reminder that the medium of the literary artist is language.

9. Williamson, Thames. "The Novelist's Use of Dialect," The Writer, XLVII (January, 1935), 3-28, 40.

Williamson says that since the basic purpose of the novel is to arouse feeling in the reader, it is foolish for the novelist to use language that is unintelligible. He discusses the dialect he uses in his own novel The Woods Colt and shows how he tried to make the language understandable. This he does by substituting a familiar word or expression for the less familiar, by allowing the context to help explain the meaning, by choosing clichés and spellings carefully, by using as little eliding as possible, by using think and know sparingly to avoid overusing reckon. Williamson says that in a dialect novel there must be naturalness and the conversation does not have to be logical and consistent. "Dialect is like garlic. A little of it is sometimes very fine, too much of it is horrible."

WRITING ASSIGNMENTS

1. Write a paper in which you analyze the use of imagery in Henry James's story, "The Great Good Place."

2. Write a paper in which you analyze the rural Florida dialect in Marjorie Kinnan Rawlings's story, "A Plumb Clare Conscience."

   3. Select one of <u>The Federalist Papers</u> and write a paper in which you compare its language and content with a present-day political speech.

"History has its rules, though they are not always followed even by professional historians; poetry, too, has its laws. The two are not necessarily irreconcilable."

--Margaret Yourcenar, "Author's Note," in Hadrian Memoirs. Garden City, N.Y.: Doubleday and Company, Inc. Doubleday Anchor Books, 1957, p. 305.

"... Historians have a great advantage over a novelist in that they can state a supposed fact without explaining it. A novelist, using the same fact, must explain it in order to make it clear to the reader."

--Kenneth Roberts, I Wanted to Write. Garden City, N.Y.: Doubleday and Company, 1949, p. 186.

"But he [the historian] is distinguished from the poet by this, that he seeks conscientiously to understand what has actually occurred, exactly as it was presented to view, and that the inner connection which he seeks is produced by the laws of nature which we revere as divine, eternal, incomprehensible. To the historian, the event itself, with its significance for the human mind, seems of most importance. To the poet, the highest value lies in his own invention, and out of fondness for this, he, at his convenience, changes the actual incident."

--Gustav Freytag. Technique of the Drama. An Exposition of Dramatic Composition and Art. Translated from Sixth German Edition by Elias J. MacEwan. Fourth Edition. Chicago: Scott, Foresman and Company, 1908, p. 16.

"A poem dealing with history is no more at liberty to violate what the writer takes to be the spirit of his history than it is at liberty to violate what the writer takes to be the nature of the human heart. What he takes those things to be is, of course, his ultimate gamble."

--Robert Penn Warren, "Foreword," Brother to Dragons. New York: Random House, 1953, p. xii.

"The truth is that to delineate a scene; to depict a personality; to portray a political crisis in all its urgency; to narrate a series of events, and to reconstruct the past in a manner that will enable people really to enter into it and feel the situation properly--these things not only require the art of literature in order to give form to the conception which the historian is seeking to communicate; they require something of the imagination of the literary man to shape them in the first place--to turn a bundle of documents into a resurrected personality and to see how a heap of dry facts, when properly put together, may present us with a dramatic human situation."

--Hubert Butterfield, "History as a Branch of Literature," in History and Human Relations. New York: Macmillan, 1953, p. 232.

"The novelist and the historian are seeking the same thing: the truth--not a different truth: the same truth--only they reach it, or try to reach it, by different routes. Whether the event took place in a world now gone to dust, preserved by documents and evaluated by scholarship, or in the imagination, preserved by memory and distilled by the creative process, they both want to tell us how it was: to re-create it, by their separate methods, and make it live again in the world around them."

--Shelby Foote, "Bibliographical Note," in The Civil War, a Narrative, Fort Sumter to Perryville. New York: Random House, 1958, p. 815.

"History can lend both color and verisimilitude to the novelist's tale. Likewise, within their limits, the novelist's imagination and observation can transform the recorded event into readable history."

--Otis A. Pease, Parkman's History. The Historian as Literary Artist. New Haven: Yale University Press, 1953, p. 84.

LITERATURE AND HISTORY

Literature and history are so closely related that it is impossible to separate them entirely, for both may use the same material and the quality of the completed work may be the only distinguishing element. Both must use imagination, but the historian must be basically concerned with facts although he may include his own interpretation of these facts. The writer of fiction, of poetry, or of drama is interested in producing a work of art, although an analysis of the writings of such historians as Gibbon and Foote shows that historians may be as interested in artistic effect as the literary artist. Dramatists are particularly attracted to history since the events of drama take place within a time frame and its medium is the re-enactment of these events. Poetry that is concerned with historical events may follow the patterns of historians in expressing the nature of historical truth.

1. Allen, Hervey. "History and the Novel," Atlantic, CLXXIII (1944), 119-121.
Allen says that both history and historical novels contain two kinds of truth, the factual and literal truth in the recording of actual events, people, and time, and the truth of the interpretation which the writer makes in writing about his data. They are different art forms, but they are similar in that they offer comment on the past based on the same data and they combine similar kinds of truth, factual and artistic. Facts used in historical fiction must be congenial to the kind of past the writer has decided to present. The historian is bound not to vary from a literal adherence to facts, but the novelist, since he appeals to the imagination, is under obligation to alter facts if the psychological truth demands that they be altered to produce a more significant effect. But the novelist should not commit grand larceny on history, for what people believe about the past helps to

fix their actions in the future.   Allen illustrates his ideas by
referring to his writing of The Disinherited.

2.   Aydelotte, William O.   "The Detective Story as
Historical Source," Yale Review, XXXIX (1949-1950), 76-95.
Aydelotte says that detective stories are of interest
to the historian, not because they give an accurate picture
of modern life, but because they provide information about
the people who read them.   Since the detective story presents a view of life that is agreeable and reassuring, it
persuades the reader that the world is meaningful and secure.
Aydelotte describes the three chief devices used in the detective story to achieve this end: it deals with very simple
problems; it casts a glamor on the characters and the
reader believes that they matter in the world; it introduces
the reader to a secure universe.   The detective story makes
the world simple, comprehensible, and orderly, and provides
security, certainty, and protection.   It creates in the reader
a feeling that he is intelligent and by following the steps in
the analysis he has somehow displayed intellectual proficiency.
Aydelotte says that the historical value of the detective story
is that it describes day-dreams.   "A knowledge of people's
day-dreams will enable us to progress to an understanding of
their desires.   In this way, a careful study of literature of
this kind may reveal attitudes which shed a flood of light on
the motivation behind political, social, and economic history."

3.   Bell, Michael Davitt.   "The Young Minister and
the Puritan Fathers: A Note on History in The Scarlet
Letter," in The Nathaniel Hawthorne Journal, 1971.   Edited
by C. E. Frazer Clark, Jr.   Dayton, Ohio: The National
Cash Register Company.   Microcard Edition, 1971, pp. 159-
167.
Although The Scarlet Letter is not based on actual
historical events, Bell says that it does use history as a
background.   In this article he points out the historical
personages used to represent different aspects of Puritan
society and says that Dimmesdale is a young minister trying
to escape the domination of the Puritan fathers.

4.   Blake, Nelson Manfred.   "Fiction as History,"
in Novelists' America, Fiction as History, 1910-1940.
Syracuse, N.Y.:   Syracuse University, 1969, pp. 254-265.
Blake says that it would be possible to learn much
about American history of the early twentieth century from
fiction alone, but this would not be the whole truth.   If the
scholar of the future would add to his library of novels facts

from such a book as <u>Historical Statistics of the United States,</u>
what then? The historian would not want to be restricted to
either the truths of the statistician or the truths of the novelist. He must speculate on the significance of events, but
he realizes that the writer of fiction uses his imagination.
The historian must also use his imagination in seeing patterns of meaning in past occurrences. Despite these similarities, the roles of the historian and of the novelist are
different. The historian's imagination must be disciplined;
the novelist, through selection and arrangement, hopes to
produce a work of art. The historian can draw upon many
sources, for to write a well-rounded view of the past he will
need to use all of the truth he can find.

5. Bond, Harold L. <u>The Literary Art of Edward
Gibbon.</u> Oxford: The Clarendon Press, 1960. 168 pp.
Bond provides a detailed analysis of the literary art
of Edward Gibbon as it is shown in <u>The Decline and Fall of
the Roman Empire.</u> The study is divided into eight chapters
concerned with the following topics: The Conception, The
Argument, The Structure, Narrative, Characters, Satire,
Language, Conclusion. Bond concludes at the close of the
chapter on "Structure" that history presented to Gibbon, as
it does to any historian, a great mass of raw material, but
Gibbon alone determined the shape and pattern of the work.
"It is not so much the fact that one man was able to assimilate such a great quantity of detail that impresses us. It is
rather the power of the mind that reduced this huge mass to
order and coherence." The chapter on "Language" discusses
the details of Gibbon's prose style: the structure of the
sentences, the use of metaphor and simile, his interest in
sounds, and the rhythms of his prose.

6. Brooks, Cleanth. "History, Tragedy, and the
Imagination in <u>Absalom, Absalom!</u>" <u>Yale Review,</u> LII (March,
1963), 340-351.
Brooks says that since in <u>Absalom, Absalom!</u> two
young men of the twentieth century try to understand the
story of Thomas Sutpen, the founder of Sutpen's Hundred, in
the period before, during, and immediately after the Civil
War, the novel is concerned with the nature of historical
truth and of how we can know the past. It is also concerned
with the defeat and guilt of the South. Brooks quotes from
Vann Woodward's <u>The Burden of Southern History:</u> "The experience of evil and the experience of tragedy are parts of
the Southern heritage that are as difficult to reconcile with
the American legend of innocence and social felicity as the

experience of poverty and defeat are to reconcile with the legends of abundance and success."

7. Driver, Tom F. "Drama and History," in The Sense of History in Greek and Shakespearean Drama. New York: Columbia University Press. Paperback Edition, 1967, pp. 3-18. Originally published in book form in 1960.
Driver says that playwrights have been attracted to history, for the theater has as its subject matter events taking place within an assumed frame of reference, and as its medium the re-enactment of these events. Driver traces the different meanings of history and shows the relation of history to the art of drama. He says that "parallels, affinities, and mutual influences do exist between dramatic and historical thinking," that both are concerned with events as objective data and as human thought and feeling, and that both are concerned with discovering meanings and patterns in the events.

8. Foote, Shelby. "The Novelist's View of History," Mississippi Quarterly, XVII (Winter, 1963-Fall, 1964), 219-225.
Foote, both a novelist and a historian, says that the novelist and the historian are seeking the same truth, but that they try to reach it by different routes. They both want to recreate the event, the historian by facts and the novelist by sensation. Foote thinks that the historian and the novelist have much to offer each other and that the historian can learn much from the novelist in matters of technique. In technique, he includes style, both the command of language and a way of looking at the world. Foote thinks that the historian errs most often in the treatment of character, in selecting material to present his views, and in his lack of sympathy for his characters. Sometimes this lack of sympathy may cause the reader to sympathize with the character because of the author's constant mistreatment. Foote says that plot is the most important element in dramatic composition, in which form he includes history. It is more than mere arrangement of events, for it concerns the amount of space and stress accorded each event; it determines what is to be left out as well as what is to be included. He thinks that the historian can learn from painting and music as well as from fiction, for all art has mutual elements, and the historian should be an artist.

9. Griffith, John. "Narrative Technique and the Meaning of History in Benét and MacLeish," The Journal of Narrative Techniques, III (January, 1973), 3-17.

Griffith discusses the debate of American historians
at the end of the last century and the beginning of the
twentieth over the nature of historical truth and the historian's discipline. On one side were the followers of Herbert
Baxter Adams, who had brought to American universities the
German ideals of objectivity and scientific detachment; on the
other side were those historians who contended that historical
truth is relative to the point of view of the truth-seeker. To
this group belonged Frederick Jackson Turner, James Harvey
Robinson, Carl Becker, and Charles Beard. At the height
of the controversy, appeared Stephen Vincent Benét's John
Brown's Body (1927) and Archibald MacLeish's Conquistador
(1932), both poems concerned with history. In this article,
Griffith discusses Benét's poem as belonging with the scientific historians, and MacLeish's poem as representative of
the other school.

10. Havard, William C. "The Burden of the Literary
Mind: Some Meditations on Robert Penn Warren as a Historian," South Atlantic Quarterly, LXII (1963), 516-531.
Havard says that Warren is not a historical novelist
but a novelist who uses history as fundamental to philosophical understanding as it is expressed through the creative
imagination. He thinks that Warren's central problem in
his novels is the self-understanding of the individual. This
comes about through the individual's experience with evil.
Havard identifies Warren's characters by placing them into
three groups according to their moral levels: those characters so dominated by pride that they seem to be lacking in
moral sensitivity, the characters who fail to grasp the relation between the evils of the world and the inner conflict
between good and evil in the individual, and the morally
mature man whose excellence introduces order into society.
He relates Warren's views of history to these ideas by referring to his biography of John Brown, The Legacy of the
Civil War, and Segregation. Havard says that the experience
of the Civil War forces self-identification both in individuals
and in the nation. "Here again is the central theme of the
search for identity, followed by a moral confrontation forced
by tragedy, and eventuating in a moral awareness which provided the potential for matured self-interpretation."

11. Hersey, John. "The Novel of Contemporary
History," Atlantic Monthly, CLXXXIV (1949), 80, 82, 84.
Reprinted in The Writer's Book. Edited by Helen Hull.
New York: Harper and Brothers, 1950, pp. 24-30.
Hersey says that the things "we remember for longer

periods are emotions and illusions and images of characters: the elements of fiction." Thus we are more apt to
remember history from reading novels about the events than
from reading historical accounts. He says that since fiction
is not as afraid of complexity as is journalism, it can deal
with the confusion of the present time; in fact, it is not
necessarily a disadvantage for a novelist to be confused provided he has discipline as a writer. "Journalism allows its
readers to witness history; fiction gives its readers an opportunity to live it." Hersey says that the motivations for
a novelist of contemporary history are a search for understanding, a desire for communication, anger directed against
a recognizable object, and a will for world citizenship. He
warns the writer of contemporary fiction not to use the
writing of a novel as a means of exposing his own inner
turmoil, and he says that any novel of contemporary events
written solely for making money will be a bad novel.

12. Literature and History. Edited by I. E. Cadenhead, Jr. Monograph Series, No. 9. Tulsa, Okla.: University of Tulsa, 1970. 102 pp. (Paper)
A series of eight papers on literature and history,
planned as a symposium, but delivered as part of the inaugu-
ration of J. Paschal Twyman as the President of the University. The following papers are included: "History and
Literature: Introduction" by I. E. Cadenhead, Jr.; "Literature as History: The Dime Novel as an Historian's Tool" by
William A. Settle, Jr.; "History as Literature: Edward
Channing's History of the United States as Literature" by
David D. Joyce; "Literature in History: The Role of the
Theater during the French Revolution" by David M. Epstein;
"History in Literature: Eugene O'Neill's Strange Interlude
as a Transcript of America in the 1920's" by Otis W. Win-
chester; "Literature to History: Exploring a Medieval Saint's
Legend and Its Context" by James I. Miller; "History to
Literature: Alternatives to History in Modern Irish Litera-
ture" by James H. Mathews; "Literature and History:
Harper's Monthly--the Magazine and the Popularization of
Knowledge" by John G. L. Dowgray, Jr.

13. Neff, Emery. The Poetry of History. The
Contribution of Literature and Literary Scholarship to the
Writing of History Since Voltaire. New York: Columbia
University Press, 1947. Columbia Paperback Edition, 1961.
258 pp.
This is the fourth in a series of books designed to
break down the compartments of literature, history, science,

social studies, and philosophy, and "to show the interdependence of ideas, events, and art." It is organized to show how literature and literary scholarship, together with political events, science, and industry, have affected the spirit, form, and content of historical writing since Voltaire. "Part One: Perspectives Open" is concerned with the work of Voltaire, Herder and Goethe, Gibbon and Vico. "Part Two: The Fulfillment" concerns Niebuhr, Otfried Müller, Chateaubriand, Scott, Thierry, and Carlyle; Michelet; Renan, Burckhardt, Green; "Part Three: Toward a New Synthesis" deals with history as science and twentieth-century thought.

14. Wedgwood, C. V. "Literature as Background Evidence for History," in Chaos and Form. History and Literature. Ideas and Relationships. Essays Selected and Edited by Kenneth McRobbie. Winnipeg, Canada: University of Manitoba Press, 1972, pp. 1-6.

Wedgwood cites Burckhardt as one of the historians who have used literature as an aid in historical research. She says that in order to understand any past incident or any past age, at a level deeper than chronological sequence and surface events, we must investigate the society that produced it. For this purpose, literature is of great value, both for incidental information and for the intellectual and moral climate. But the modern historian is so burdened with essential research that he may neglect the literature. "Yet, even allowing for limitations, there is no better way of acquiring the necessary familiarity with a section of the past, with its ideas and outlook, than prolonged immersion in its literature. This familiarity, this 'sense of the period' as it is often called, is something that the historian must acquire if he is to get the full value out of his more direct historical sources."

15. Williams, Ben Ames. "Fiction's Fourth Dimension," The Saturday Review of Literature, XXI (October 16, 1948), 8-9, 32-33.

Williams calls the historical element in fiction its "fourth-dimensional" quality and says that there is no such thing as a non-historical novel, for every novel is a contribution to history. A writer of historical fiction must know the material that he writes about or the reader will recognize his ignorance. He must investigate authentic source materials--published contemporary documents, unpublished letters and diaries, newspaper accounts--and he must know the social and economic picture of the time. To learn how people talk today, the writer can listen to phonograph recordings and broadcasts, but the author writing of the past must be careful to choose language suitable to the period. Williams says that historical novels give the reader a wider knowledge of the past than do most textbooks in American history, a knowledge that helps him to understand the present. "The text of every sound historical novel is the same. There is no past; the past is now."

16. Williams, Wirt. "Shelby Foote's Civil War: The Novelist as Humanistic Historian," Mississippi Quarterly, XXIV (Fall, 1971), 429-436.
    Williams says that history becomes literature when it is well written. This he calls "humanistic history," history that has literary art as one of its dimensions. In this category, Williams places Shelby Foote's The Civil War: A Narrative, for in it, he says, Foote has merged the methods of responsible history with the resources of the art of the novelist. (Williams bases his statements on the first two volumes, the only volumes published at this time.) Williams finds in the Narrative seven parallels with both fiction and drama: the narrative develops in the alternation between the protagonist (the South) and the antagonist (the Union); in the case of the protagonist the thrust matures into formal tragedy; each of the two forces is represented by human leaders; great attention is paid to the development of the characters; the method of narration follows essentially the method of fiction; the scenes are presented much as a novelist presents scenes; language is used as an esthetic component.

17. Wilson, Edmund. "The Historical Interpretation of Literature," in The Triple Thinkers. New York: Oxford University Press, 1938, 1948. Galaxy Book, 1963, pp. 257-270.
    In this lecture, Wilson discusses the "non-historical" criticism of T. S. Eliot and George Saintsbury, the social interpretation of literature by Vico and Dr. Johnson, and the ideas of Herder, who thought of national literature as expressions of the societies that produced them. The historical point of view, says Wilson, reached its height in Taine's pronouncement that works of literature are the result of three factors: the moment, the race, and the milieu. Marx and Engels introduced the economic element. But the insistence that the man of letters should play a political role came in Russia from the censorship of Nicholas I. The Russians thought that art must be technically objective but charged with social messages. Then came the psychoanalysis techniques of

Freud. But these historical and biographical points of view
do not help in distinguishing good literature from bad.
Wilson's own criterion of literary art comes from the statement of Norman Kemp Smith, who says that the recognition
of what is good is based primarily on an emotional reaction.
Wilson says that all intellectual activity is an attempt to
give meaning to our experience. "With each such victory of
the human intellect, whether in history, in philosophy, or in
poetry, we experience a deep satisfaction: we have been
cured of some ache of disorder, relieved of some oppressive
burden of uncomprehended events." This relief tells us that
we have encountered a first-rate piece of literature.

WRITING ASSIGNMENTS

1. In the "Foreword" to Brother to Dragons, Random
House, 1953, Robert Penn Warren gives the historical basis
of his long poem. Read this account and the poem and write
a paper in which you discuss Warren's use of history and the
changes he made in using this material in the poem. Point
out both omissions and additions and explain the reasons for
both. You may want to examine recent biographies of Jefferson to determine whether he made any reference to this
episode in his family history.

2. Several articles have been written on Robert Penn
Warren's use of history in his poetry, fiction, and essays.
Read one of his novels and write a paper in which you point
out his use of history in the novel. You may also need to
read a recent history of the events covered by the novel.

3. Read Chapter II of Look Back to Glory, 1933, by
Herbert Ravenel Sass, and write a paper in which you compare his account of the Battle of Fort Sumter as given by a
novelist with the account given by an historian such as
Shelby Foote. Point out the differences in the ways a novelist and a historian handle the same material.

4. Read one of the selections in History as Literature,
edited and with an introduction by Orville Prescott (New York
and Evanston: Harper and Row, 1970), and write a paper in
which you point out and discuss the literary qualities of the
historical selection. Or, write a paper in which you group
the selections according to the subjects treated and discuss
the topics that may be treated in historical accounts. Or,
using the biographical material included in the volume, write

a paper in which you show the relation between biography and history.

5. Read Caroline Gordon's story, "The Captive" in Contemporary Southern Prose, edited by Richmond Croom Beatty and William Perry Fidler, D. C. Heath, 1940, pp. 470-508, and the historical account on which it is based, The Founding of Harman's Station with an Account of the Indian Captivity of Mrs. Jennie Wiley and the Exploration and Settlement of the Big Sandy Valley in the Virginias and Kentucky by William Esley Connelley, New York, 1910, and write a paper in which you show how Caroline Gordon as a writer of fiction uses and adapts history to her purpose. You should also read "Caroline Gordon and 'The Captive': An Interview, " by Catherine B. Baum and Floyd C. Watkins, in Southern Review, VII (1971), 447-462.

6. Make a study of the use of history in one of Maxwell Anderson's plays: Valley Forge, 1934; Elizabeth the Queen, 1930; Mary Queen of Scotland, 1933. You may want to relate the situation in the United States when Valley Forge was written to the situation that is presented in the play. Write a concluding paragraph on the relation between history and drama. You may write a similar paper on T. S. Eliot, Murder in the Cathedral, 1935.

7. Write a paper in which you show how Shakespeare used history in one of his plays. The Sources of Ten Shakespearean Plays by Alice Griffin, 1966, provides the sources of a play you may want to use.

8. Read An American Tragedy by Theodore Dreiser, or In Cold Blood by Truman Capote and newspaper accounts of the murder or murders upon which each is based, and write a paper in which you show how the actual can be transposed into the fictional.

9. Read the account of Samson in the Book of Judges and Milton's account in Samson Agonistes and write a paper in which you discuss the use that Milton made of his source. How much did he use? How much omit? What changes did he make?

10. Write a paper in which you present the portrait of the historical scholar in Willa Cather's novel, The Professor's House.

"Literary art, it seems to me, is the most personal creation of man: it is the use of words to express feeling and experience in story and poem, in metaphor and simile. Far from ignoring the life of an artist, ... we must encounter that life in the artist's work. We can hardly avoid it, for the work is a kind of supreme biography of the artist: it is by his work that the artist asserts himself, and writes his name, his voice, his style--his and no one else's--into the memory of men."

--Leon Edel, "Willa Cather," in Literary Lectures. Presented at the Library of Congress. Washington, D.C.: Library of Congress, 1973, pp. 355-356.

LITERATURE AND BIOGRAPHY

1. Armstrong, William A. "History, Autobiography, and The Shadow of a Gunman," Modern Drama, II (February, 1960), 417-424.
    Armstrong says that a comparison of The Shadow of a Gunman with certain parts of O'Casey's autobiography, Inishfallen, Fare Thee Well (1949) shows that the personal element in the play is more important than the historical element since it helped to determine the form and interpretation of life the play represents. Armstrong points out the items of local geography and history O'Casey uses in the play and items in the play that parallel items in the autobiography. He also points out differences in the play and in the autobiography, especially the substitution of Minnie Powell for Mr. Ballynog.

2. Edel, Leon. "Literature and Biography," in Relations of Literary Study. Essays on Interdisciplinary Contributions. Edited by James Thorpe. New York: Modern Language Association, 1965, pp. 57-72.
    Edel argues that literature and biography are closely related, for the study of one involves the study of the other. The new biography, the writings, criticism, and psychoanalysis are all means of arriving at an understanding of the writer and none should be excluded. "All art ... is personal and impersonal at the same time. We can most truthfully study literature when we link the poem to the poet." Thus literary biography which deals exclusively with the writer's life is incomplete. Edel says that modern criticism is so "inundated with personal reading of texts" that biographical and historical evidence are necessary to prevent "critical anarchy." He thinks that in revealing the writer within the work the biographer removes some of the mystery of the writer, but he compensates by providing a picture of achievement and triumph, and thus knowledge and insight are gained.

3. Edel, Leon. "The Novel as Autobiography," in
The Modern Psychological Novel. New York: Grove Press,
Inc. Evergreen Books, 1955, pp. 103-122.
Edel divides the discussion into four sections. In
section one, he uses Henry James and Marcel Proust to illustrate how memory is used by James for autobiography and by
Proust for fiction. In the second section, Edel compares the
fragment of Stephen Hero, the materials of which Joyce
worked into the last chapter of A Portrait of the Artist as a
Young Man, with the incomplete novel, Jean Santeuil, found
among Proust's papers and published in three volumes. Both
are autobiographical. In section three, Edel says that in the
technical sense Proust is writing autobiographical fiction, but
in the larger sense he has created art independent of its
creator, as Joyce does in Ulysses. In section four, Edel
says that both Proust and Joyce reach the conclusion that although fictional characters begin in the first person, they can
end in the third, while their creator removes himself into
anonymity. But Edel concludes that there still remains a
quality of mind that informs a work even though the artist
has disengaged himself.

4. Kazin, Alfred. "Autobiography as Narrative," in
To the Young Writer. Hopwood Lectures, Second Series.
Edited by A. L. Bader. Ann Arbor: University of Michigan
Press. Ann Arbor Paperbacks, 1965, pp. 181-193.
"Autobiography, like other literary forms," says
Kazin, "is what a gifted writer makes of it." In this lecture,
Kazin discusses autobiography as fiction, "that is, as narrative which has no purpose other than to tell a story, to
create the effect of a story." Autobiography as narrative
seeks the effect of fiction, but it uses facts as strategy.
The difference between formal fiction and autobiography is
that autobiography is centered on a single person. Kazin
attributes the present interest in autobiography to the interest
in the self. He says that it is an authentic way of establish-
ing the truth of our experience.

5. Stone, Irving. "The Biographical Novel," in The
Irving Stone Reader. Originally published by Doubleday and
Company, 1963. Freeport, N.Y.: Books for Libraries
Press, 1971, pp. 12-30.
Irving Stone defines the biographical novel as "a true
and documented story of one human being's journey across
the face of the years, transmuted from the raw materials of
life into the delight and purity of an authentic art form." It
attempts to fuse biography and the novel with history, but it

must follow the structure of the novel. Stone says that history is the master of the biographical novelist and no biographical novel can be better than the research involved. Personal and professional integrity are necessary, for the biographical novel provides as much a portrait of the author as of the subject, and it can be no better than the mind of the author. The biographical novelist must be trained as a biographer, as a writer of fiction, and as a researcher. Stone gives an outline of how a biographical novelist should work, and he refers to his own novels for illustrations.

6. Wellek, René, and Austin Warren. "Literature and Biography," in Theory of Literature. New York: Harcourt, Brace and World, Inc. Harvest Book Edition, 1956, pp. 63-68.

Wellek and Warren say that biography can be judged in relation to the light it throws on the actual production of poetry, can be justified as a study of a man of genius, and can provide material for a systematic study of the poet and of the poetic process. The first point of view uses biography to explain the actual product of poetry. The second shifts the attention to personality. The third is concerned with artistic creation. The authors raise and answer two questions about literary biography. How far is the biographer justified in using a writer's works? How far are the results of literary biography important for an understanding of the works themselves? Their answer to the first question is negative. They reply to the second question that biographical study may be of some use in studying an author's works. It may explain words or allusions in the works; it may help to show the writer's development; and it may provide material for literary history.

WRITING ASSIGNMENTS

1. Write a paper in which you compare the interpretation of Shakespeare as it is given in a biography with that of Edwin Arlington Robinson's characterization in "Ben Jonson Entertains a Man from Stratford."

2. Read Irving Stone's The Agony and the Ecstasy, a Biographical Novel of Michelangelo, 1961, and a recent biography of Michelangelo and compare the portraits of Michelangelo as given in the two works.

3. Read Irving Stone's essay on "The Biographical

Novel" and one of his biographical novels and write a paper
in which you show how he carried out his ideas in the novel.
Choose any one of his novels: Lust for Life, 1934; Immortal
Wife, 1944; The President's Lady, 1951; Love Is Eternal,
1954; The Agony and the Ecstasy, 1961; The Greek Treasure,
1975.

    4.   Read Harry Williams' Huey Long and Robert Penn
Warren's novel, All the King's Men, 1946, and write a paper
in which you discuss Warren's use of biography in his novel.
You may want to read Robert B. Heilman's "Williams on
Long: The Story Itself," Southern Review, VI (Summer-
Autumn, 1970), 935-953, and Robert Penn Warren's All the
King's Men: The Matrix of Experience," Yale Review, LII
(December, 1963), 161-167. Or, you may use Stephen Crane,
a Biography by Robert W. Stallman, 1968, and Louis Zara,
The Dark Rider: A Novel Based on the Life of Stephen
Crane, 1961.

"'These,' said the lawyer Pleydell, showing his fine collection of classical authors, 'are my tools of trade. A lawyer without history or literature is a mechanic, a mere working mason; if he possesses some knowledge of these he may venture to call himself an architect.'"

--Walter Scott, quoted in Gilbert Highet, "Prose of the Law," in Explorations. New York: Oxford University Press, 1971, p. 340.

LITERATURE AND LAW

That law has a fascination for writers is shown by the large number of novelists, dramatists, and poets who have used some aspect of law in their works. A study of legal documents is also important in uncovering facts of biography.

1. Anderson, Dillon. "From Law to Literature," Southwest Review, XL (Summer, 1955), 249-254.
     A humorous account of how a lawyer in Texas became a writer of stories in addition to his practice of law. He draws some conclusions about the similarities between legal writing and the writing of fiction: the satisfaction of reducing an idea to words, finding the right word to fit the thought, the "fun" of sentence revision, the development of a series of thoughts and ideas in logical and orderly sequence. He also points out some differences: a lawyer does not make facts but deals with what the client brings; in writing fiction, the sky is the limit. In law practice one must follow rules and regulations; the fiction writer is not bound by decrees and may write as he pleases. Anderson's conclusion is that one has to like writing, for the work is too difficult unless one really wants to write. "It's heady stuff to start with a blank sheet of paper and wind up weeks or months later with people spun from dreams."

2. Hotson, J. Leslie. The Death of Christopher Marlowe. New York: Haskell House, 1965. 76 pp. Originally published by Nonesuch Press, 1925.
     An account of how Hotson uncovered the mystery of the death of Christopher Marlowe by examining the public records of 1593, the time of Marlowe's death. Hotson located a copy of the Queen's pardon to Ingram Frizer for the murder of Marlowe and a copy of the findings of the coroner's jury.

3. Pottle, Frederick A. "Notes on the Importance of Private Legal Documents for the Writing of Biography and Literary History," Proceedings of the American Philosophical Society, CVI, No. 4 (August 22, 1962), 327-334.

Pottle illustrates his statements about the importance of private legal documents in literary scholarship by referring to his work in uncovering the deed of James Boswell which gave his daughter Veronica five hundred pounds on March 3, 1795, an item which made an important addition to the biography of Boswell. Pottle suggests that a scholar who wants to find out whether a family has legal papers that he ought to see should engage a good lawyer to treat with the family solicitor.

4. Wigmore, John H. "A List of One Hundred Legal Novels," in Voices in Court: A Treasury of the Bench, the Bar, and the Courtroom. Edited by William H. Davenport. New York: Macmillan Company, 1958, pp. 583-585.

WRITING ASSIGNMENTS

1. Read one of the one hundred legal novels listed in Voices in Court: A Treasury of the Bench, the Bar, and the Courtroom, edited by William H. Davenport, 1958, pp. 583-585, and write a paper in which you present the legal aspects of the novel.

2. Write a paper in which you compare the trial of John Brown in Erlich's Life of John Brown with the trial in Stephen Vincent Benét's John Brown's Body. Or, compare the trial of Jesus in Anatole France's The Procurator of Judea with that in Judas Iscariot by Stephen Spender.

3. Read The Ring and the Book by Robert Browning and write a paper in which you discuss the legal aspects of the poem. Or, write a paper in which you discuss Browning's use of his source, an account of an actual murder. Read Curious Annals: New Documents Relating to Browning Roman Murder Story, translated and edited by Beatrice Corrigan, University of Toronto Press, 1956. See also The Old Yellow Book, Everyman Edition, arranged and edited by Charles S. Hedell, as well as the account in Browning Handbook by W. C. DeVane.

"My mind seems to have become a kind of machine
for grinding general laws out of large collections of facts,
but why this should have caused the atrophy of that part of
the brain alone, on which the higher tastes depend, I cannot
conceive. A man with a mind more highly organized or
better constituted than mine, would not, I suppose, have thus
suffered; and if I had to live my life again, I would have made
a rule to read some poetry and listen to some music at least
once every week; for perhaps the parts of my brain now atro-
phied would thus have been kept active through use. The loss
of these tastes is a loss of happiness, and may possibly be
injurious to the intellect, and more probably to the moral
character, by enfeebling the emotional part of our nature."

--Charles Darwin's Autobiography. Edited by Francis
Darwin. New York: Henry Schuman, 1950, pp. 66-67.

LITERATURE AND SCIENCE

Except for particular scientific terms and the use of
scientific formulas, there is little difference in the writing
of science and literature; in fact, some of the best scientific
writing has literary value. The collection of interdisciplinary
essays included in this section is designed to broaden the
study of literature by showing the values in other disciplines.

1. Keller, A. G. "What Literature Can Do for
Science," Yale Review, XXXX (1941), 560-565.
Keller begins with a discussion of the importance of
the study of literature on the writing of scientists, but nar-
rows his discussion to its effect on social scientists. He
thinks that the way to learn to write is to acquire a feeling
for words and style and by practicing what the masters
preach through observing what they practice. He believes
that the teacher of any science should learn to write a decent
style himself and then refuse credit to students who do not
themselves learn to express their ideas in "stylistic decency."
Keller illustrates his remarks by referring to literary writers,
particularly Homer.

2. Sawyer, Thomas M. "The Common Law of Science
and The Common Law of Literature," College Composition and
Communication, XXXI (December, 1970), 337-341.
Sawyer says that since science and literature are both
products of the human mind, it is difficult to determine
whether some works should be considered as literature or
as scientific studies. The division, he says, is primarily
one of rhetoric. But some of the sciences, such as physics,
may use a language that creates a gap. Sawyer accepts
F. S. C. Northop's idea that as long as a science is in the
natural history stage, it is logically compatible with art. The
scientist and the artist view the world in the same way. Late
the scientist imposes upon the world of sense impressions what

156

Northrop calls "concepts of perception." Since it is the business of the scientist to predict the future, he must employ causal relationships and these are difficult to translate into terms that are understood by the nonscientist. When the literary man goes beyond the stage of pure observation, he goes through the same abstractive process as does the scientist. He superimposes an abstract and symbolic meaning on what is sensed. He uses these concepts for the same reason the scientist does: "to create a deductive system which will enable us to predict what will follow when men act toward other men in a specified way in a specified situation."

3. Science and Literature. New Lenses for Criticism. Edited by Edward M. Jennings. Garden City, N.Y.: Doubleday and Company, Inc. Anchor Books Edition, 1970. 262 pp. (Paper)
This collection of interdisciplinary essays is designed to broaden the study of literature by showing the values in other disciplines. The editor's idea of "interdisciplinary" study "involves the adaptation, by practitioners in one academic specialty, of methods and attitudes associated with another." The significant integration of different disciplinary attitudes, he says, cannot be accomplished by interdepartmental or problem-centered courses. There are fourteen essays in the collection, each independent, but related to the others. They include essays on such topics as the nature of language, plot analysis, a theory about theories, and the application of computer science and modern linguistics to literary studies.

WRITING ASSIGNMENTS

1. Read Paul de Kruif's account of the writing of Arrowsmith in The Sweeping Wind (New York: Harcourt, Brace and World, Inc., 1962), pp. 54-119, and compare his account with that given by Mark Schorer in Sinclair Lewis: An American Life (New York: McGraw-Hill Book Company, Inc., 1961), pp. 338-40, 364-69, 406-07, 419-20. De Kruif collaborated with Sinclair Lewis on the novel, providing medical material for the novel, but his name does not appear as co-author. He received one-fourth of the proceeds. De Kruif's book as a whole is a good example of writing about scientific subjects for popular reading. It also provides insights into how one becomes a writer.

2. Read "Great Northern Diver or Loon," in The Birds of America by John James Audubon, Jr. (New York: Dover Publications, 1967), VII, 282-294, and Thoreau's account of the loon in "Brute Neighbors" in Walden, and write a paper in which you compare the ways by which a scientist and a literary writer handle the same material. Compare not only subject matter but language and style as well. Or, you may use Charles Darwin, The Voyage of the Beagle, edited by Leonard Engel (New York: Doubleday and Company; Anchor Books, 1962), pp. 383-390, in which Darwin describes the tortoises on the Galapagos Archipelago, and compare this account with Herman Melville's in The Encantadas, Sketch Second, "Two Sides to a Tortoise."

LITERATURE, HISTORY, AND SCIENCE

1. Daiches, David. "Literature, History, and Science," in A Study of Literature for Readers and Critics. New York: W. W. Norton and Company, Inc. Norton Library Edition, 1948, pp. 90-107.

Daiches says that novels are popular because only a few people take them seriously. But the fact that history or philosophy or social criticism may be disguised as fiction does not mean that it has value as imaginative literature. History can be a science in that it communicates established facts, but the formulation of historical generalizations is largely an act of the imagination. History tends toward art to the degree that language is used in such a way as to expand the events and characters described into something more than historical symbols. If the historian expands his comments beyond his subject matter, he tends to become an artist as well as an historian. If he makes this expansion by explicit generalization, he is acting as a philosopher. If his material emerges as a result of the way he uses language, he is acting as a literary artist. The difference between good history and good fiction is a difference in the degree to which the imagination works through language. The fiction writer who uses historical material imposes a pattern on his material which derives from his sense of significance as an artist. Daiches thinks that literary studies and scientific studies can help each other. "The literary craftsmanship which is not itself art but is a prerequisite for art affects the very quality of our civilization--the way we think, the kind of expression we give to our thoughts, the extent to which we recognize confused thought in others." The ability to use language becomes of direct importance to the scientist only when he wishes to talk about scientific situations, not to present them. Appreciation of the way something is expressed is only possible when the kind of subject to be expressed demands expressions through a medium richer and subtler than a formula.

2. Toynbee, Arnold J. "History, Science and Fiction," in The Philosophy of History in Our Time. Selected and Edited by Hans Meyerhoff. Garden City, N.Y.: Doubleday and Company, Inc. Doubleday Anchor Books, 1959, pp. 114-119.

Toynbee says that there are three different methods of viewing and presenting ideas. The first is the obtaining and the recording of facts; the second is the statement of general laws; the third is the re-creation of the facts in the form of fiction. It is generally assumed that the first belongs to the technique of history, the second to the technique of science, and the third to the techniques of drama and the novel. But he says that there may be an overlapping. History does not record all of the facts and may use the techniques of science and fiction. Science and fiction do not confine themselves to their own techniques. The techniques differ in their use of handling different quantities of data. If the data happen to be few, the techniques of history apply. If the data are too numerous to tabulate, the formulation of laws is necessary. If the data are innumerable, the only techniques that can be used are those of fiction.

HISTORY AND OTHER DISCIPLINES

HISTORY AND BIOGRAPHY

1. Heilman, Robert B. "Williams on Long: The
Story Itself, " Southern Review, VI (Summer-Autumn, 1970),
935-953.
Heilman discusses Harry Williams' Huey Long from
the viewpoint of one who lived in Louisiana for twelve years
and who was present in the visitors' gallery of the Louisiana
Legislature the day that Long was shot. He thinks that
Williams' biographic art is in the story itself. He says that
Williams uses the techniques of fiction and drama and min-
gles the serious business of history with the histrionics of
Louisiana politics. He discusses the character and the situation of Huey Long and relates Williams' account to his own
interpretations. Williams raises many questions about Long:
Was he a "power artist, " a picaresque hero, a low-comedy
character, a melodramatic villain, a tragic hero, an ego-
maniac? Heilman concludes that Long's challenge to the
imagination is great. "He died young, but he makes a strong
impact on the psychic centers from which flow the arts of
historical and literary interpretation. "

2. Nevins, Allan. "The Biographer and the Historian, " in The Humanities for Our Time. Edited by Walter
R. Agard and Others. University of Kansas Lectures in the
Humanities. Lawrence: University of Kansas Press, 1949,
pp. 45-66.
Nevins says that history and biography are so closely
related that no one can be a good historian without being in
part a biographer, and no one can be a biographer without
being partially an historian. He divides biographies into
three types: the portrait stripped of all unnecessary detail,
in which the materials have been passed through the mind
of the author and appear in a concentrated state, the life
proper; the monumental life and letters; the biography which

161

presents the hero in his full historical setting, the life, letters, and time. The last type, he says, has been criticized for its mixture of biography and history in which the figure may be lost to view. Nevins says that biography aids history in two ways: by the discovery and presentation of facts, and by the interpretation of a man, either alone or in relation to his times. Biography also adds a humanizing quality to history.

3. Nevins, Allan. "Biography and History," in The Gateway to History. Garden City, N.Y.: Doubleday and Company, Inc. New, revised edition. Anchor Books, 1962, pp. 347-369.

Nevins says that the popularity of biography over history is due to several factors: it humanizes the past and enriches personal experience; it simplifies what is sometimes vast and complex; it provides personal emotion instead of the impersonal view of the impartial historian. Biography provides a knowledge of individual psychology just as history provides a knowledge of social action. Biography is valuable as a study of one important form of historical force. "The chief requirement of a good biography is that it re-create an individual, convincing the reader that he lived, moved, spoke, and enjoyed a certain set of human attributes." A good biography should also present a complete, accurate, and an unbiased account of the deeds and experiences of its subject. "A great biography is a creation on the symphonic or operatic order, not a lyric."

HISTORY AND SCIENCE

1. East, W. Gordon. "Geography as an Historical Document," in The Geography Behind History. London: Thomas Nelson and Sons, Ltd., 1965, pp. 1-14.

The geographer's knowledge of the earth's surface can be applied to the past, and thus it becomes relevant to the historian. The physical aspect of geography is common to all historical periods. But morphological changes have occurred which have affected human history: volcanic eruptions and earthquakes, changes in the courses of rivers, erosions of coastlands, extensions of the deserts, etc. Geography behind history offers a partial explanation of the means of livelihood used by people in different areas. Man's achievement in changing the face of the land can be understood only if it is set against the relatively unchanging background.

2. Hawkins, Gerald S. "The Secret of Stonehenge," Harper's Magazine, CCXXVIII (June, 1964), 95-99.
Hawkins, a professor of astronomy, tells how, with the help of two assistants at the Smithsonian Astrophysical Observatory, he fed information into a computer, the results of which established the fact that the positions of the stones at Stonehenge pointed to a sun or moon rise or set. "It could have formed a reliable calendar to predict change of seasons. It could also have signaled danger periods for eclipses of the sun or moon. It could have formed a dramatic setting for observation of the interchange between the sun--dominator of summer--and the moon--ruler of winter."

3. Mackensen, H. F. "Is History a Science?" in The Humanities in the Age of Science. Edited by Charles Angoff. Madison, N.J.: Fairleigh Dickinson University Press, 1968, pp. 139-153.
Mackensen raises the question as to whether history is or is not a science and analyzes the methods of writing history in both situations by referring to the work of prominent historians. He concludes that in research the historian is a scientist; in interpretation, he is a philosopher; in presenting his findings, he is an artist.

4. Nevins, Allan. "What the Scientist and Historian Can Teach Each Other," in Allan Nevins on History. Compiled and Introduced by Ray Allen Billington. New York: Charles Scribner's Sons, 1975, pp. 133-150.
Nevins says that the great defect of science from the standpoint of the historian and the writer generally is in its lack of interest in the human spirit and emotions. History, on the other hand, has been "shallowly humanistic." Nevins says that history should be a mixture of literary and scientific elements. It needs statistics, abnormal psychology, scientific geography, biology, economics, sociology, and political theory. The historian is needed to counteract the behavioristic thinking that the individual is shaped primarily by his education and environment. Nevins thinks that when history and science are pursued with imagination, they have common points. The historian can learn from the scientist his dedication to impartial methods of study. The scientist can acquire from the historian a sense of perspective. But both the historian and the scientist need the philosopher.

"A man's power to connect his thought with its proper symbol, and so to utter it, depends on the simplicity of his character, that is, upon his love of truth and his desire to communicate it without loss. The corruption of man is followed by the corruption of language."

--Ralph Waldo Emerson, "Language," in Nature, 1836.

"Language is not merely the way we express our foreign policy; language is our foreign policy."

--Robert F. Drinan, "The Rhetoric of Peace," College Composition and Communication, XXIII (October, 1972), 279.

"It is as important for the purpose of thought to keep language efficient as it is in surgery to keep tetanus bacilli out of one's bandages."

--Ezra Pound, "How to Read," in The Literary Essays of Ezra Pound. Edited and with an Introduction by T. S. Eliot. New York: New Directions, 1968, p. 22.

"If our political language, and therefore our public thinking, becomes so debauched that moral meanings can no longer be clearly expressed or understood, then all the gadgets, technology, and techniques of Watergate will be unnecessary. We will have already slipped into a 1984 nightmare. A society that cannot speak or understand sense is condemned to live nonsensically."

--Richard Gambino, "Watergate Lingo: A Language of Non-Responsibility," in Language and Public Policy. Edited by Hugh Rank. Urbana, Illinois: National Council of Teachers of English, 1974, p. 20.

LANGUAGE AND POLITICS

Several of the writers on language emphasize the relation between dishonest and inhumane use of language and our chance of survival. There is also a relation between one's use of language and the ability to think clearly. George Orwell says that the present political chaos is connected with the decay of language, and that one can probably bring about some improvement by starting at the verbal end. He was writing in 1945.

1. Galbraith, John Kenneth. "The Language of Economics," Fortune, LXVI, No. 6 (December, 1962), 128-130, 169, 171.
Galbraith points out and answers the charges that economists do not express themselves clearly in their writing; that the concepts and terminology of economists are complex and confusing to the layman; that economists are bad writers; that the concepts and obscure language are an indication that economists are trying to construct a universe of their own. He answers the first charge by saying that the charge is not serious, as is shown by the speed with which the words and ideas of economists pass into general use. To the second charge, he points out the writing of such distinguished economists as Adam Smith, J. S. Mill, Thorstein Veblen, Malthus, Henry George, Alfred Marshall, and Lord Keynes, for whom he has reservations. He states that good writing must also involve the reader. He is also not sure that clear and unambiguous writing is an asset for persuasion in economics since the effort to understand may lead to discussion of and belief in the writer's ideas. To the third accusation, Galbraith answers that there is a prestige of structure of economists who at the higher levels divorce themselves from practical questions and other fields with the exception of mathematics and statistics. The ability to master difficult mathematical concepts is a useful device for screening the prestige economists.

2. Language and Politics. Selected Writing. Edited by Thomas P. Brockway. Boston: D. C. Heath and Company, 1965. 111 pp. (Paper)
This is a collection of selections to illustrate the uses of language for political purposes and designed to sharpen the reader's awareness of the influence of political discourse. The material, organized into nine sections, was written by statesmen and politicians as well as by established authors and journalists. The book opens with George Orwell's essay on "Politics and the English Language" and closes with Norman Cousins' "Modern Man Is Obsolete," an essay written less than two weeks after the bomb was dropped on Hiroshima.

3. Language and Public Policy. Edited by Hugh Rank. NCTE Committee on Public Doublespeak. Urbana, Illinois: National Council of Teachers of English, 1974. 248 pp. (Paper)
A collection of 36 essays and a personal reading list compiled by the editor on public doublespeak, designed to show the dishonest and inhumane uses of language and to urge teachers, especially English teachers, to teach their students to understand such verbal manipulation and to learn how to combat it. The essays are grouped into four sections: "Watergate as Watershed," "In and Out of the Classroom," "A Call to Action ... and Some Responses," "The NCTE Committee on Public Doublespeak." There is a concluding essay by the editor.

4. Language in America. Edited by Neil Postman, Charles Weingarten, and Terence P. Moran. New York: Pegasus Books. Copyright by Western Publishing Company, Inc., 1969. 240 pp.
With the subtitle of "A Report on Our Deteriorating Semantic Environment," this collection of essays is concerned with language as the key to human survival. The essays thus focus on the extent to which the language of politics, advertising, psychotherapy, education, bureaucracy, censorship, law, racism, etc., aids or hinders our chance of survival. The purpose of the book is "to make a beginning toward monitoring the language environment." There are twenty chapters, each written by an authority or authorities in the field.

5. Morse, J. Mitchell. "Composition and Politics," The CEA Critic, XXXVIII, No. 2 (January, 1976), 4-7.
Morse says that the teaching of the principles of linguistic evolution should begin early and should be continued

into college classes so that the student is not frustrated in trying to use his native language. He thinks that English teachers now have the opportunity to "intellectualize" their students so that they will not be fooled by "political admen" and "doublespeakers." This, he thinks, "would be a step toward restoring the national dignity of the United States."

6. Newman, Edwin. Strictly Speaking. Will America Be the Death of English? Indianapolis/New York: The Bobbs-Merrill Company, Inc., 1974. 205 pp.
Newman says that the state of our language is a commentary on the state of our society. Language is in decline. Not only has eloquence departed but so has simple, direct speech. He says that it is at least conceivable that if our language were improved, then politics and other parts of our national life would also improve. He illustrates his comments on the condition of the English language by referring to the language used by people in the business of using language--presidents, vice-presidents, diplomats, sportscasters, senators, newsmen, social scientists, college presidents, etc.--and especially their use of clichés, errors, and jargon. There are eight chapters in addition to the "Introduction: A Protective Interest in the English Language."

7. Orwell, George. "Politics and the English Language," in Shooting an Elephant and Other Essays. New York: Harcourt, Brace and Company, 1945, 1946, 1949, 1950, pp. 77-92.
Orwell's thesis is that there is a direct relation between one's use of language and the ability to think clearly ("the slovenliness of our language makes it easier for us to have foolish thoughts"). He says that "vagueness and sheer incompetency is the most marked characteristic of English prose, and especially of any kind of political writing." The whole tendency of modern prose is away from concreteness. It consists of "gumming together long strips of words which have already been set in order by someone else." Political language, Orwell says, is designed "to make lies sound truthful and murder respectable, and to give an appearance of solidity to pure wind." He suggests that we discard worn-out and useless language and let the meaning choose the words.

8. Schlesinger, Arthur, Jr. "Politics and the American Language," American Scholar, XLIII (Autumn, 1974), 553-562.
Schlesinger says that desire for success at the polls has cheapened the language of politics, and the corruption of

the individual through the desire for economic gains and for power has corrupted the language. The divorce of words from objects tends to divorce words from meaning. "The rise of mass communications, the growth of large organizations and novel technologies, the invention of advertising and public relations, the professionalization of education--all contributed to linguistic pollution, upsetting the ecological balance between words and their environment." The control of language is a necessary step toward the control of minds. If we are to restore the relationship between words and meaning, we must clean up the linguistic environment. The redemption of language is thus a contribution to the redemption of politics.

WRITING ASSIGNMENT

The following paragraphs were given awards by the NCTE Committee on Doublespeak, the first for its use of gobbledygook and the last two for their use of educationese. Read them carefully and then write a paper in which you comment on their "misuse" of language. The first paragraph is the reply of Ron Ziegler, press secretary to President Richard Nixon, to a question from reporters about whether a set of Watergate tapes were unchanged. The second and third paragraphs are from the presidential address of Don J. Willower of Pennsylvania State University to the University Council for Education Administration.

"I would feel that most of the conversations that took place in those areas of the White House that did have the recording system would in almost their entirety be in existence but the special prosecutor, the court, and, I think, the American people are sufficiently familiar with the recording system to know where the recording devices existed and to know the situation in terms of the recording process but I feel, although the process has not been undertaken yet in preparation of the material to abide by the court decision, really, what the answer to that question is."

"The point in all this is not that frameworks that stress the individual and commonly exhibit a psychological orientation are full of error. They are not. To the contrary, they often furnish important insights. But such modes have dominated the thinking of many educators, a state of affairs reinforced by the tangibility of the person as an object of analysis as contrasted with the misty, abstruse quality of system concepts."

"Yet, the most basic problems that arise in connection with knowledge utilization may be those that stem from the social and organizational character of educational institutions. A few university adaptations already have been highlighted. Public schools display a myriad of normative and other regulatory structures that promote internal predictability, as well as a host of adaptive mechanisms that reduce external uncertainties."

--Quoted in Public Doublespeak Newsletter, II, Number 1 (Fall, 1974), 8.

CHAPTER 7

WRITING ARTICLES FOR NEWSPAPERS AND MAGAZINES:
TRAVEL, PEOPLE, PLACES, OCCASIONS, ETC.

"It's [free-lance writing] the only business I know where the worker is compensated totally at the caprice of the customer, whether or not the customer ordered the merchandise and whether or not it was delivered in good faith and in reasonably good condition. In free-lance writing, the risks that beset any contractual arrangement between two fallible human beings are borne almost entirely by the writer."

--Joseph N. Bell, "Why Free-Lance Writers Get Nervous," Saturday Review of Literature, L (November 11, 1967), 91.

"But the book review as a literary form implies completeness; it has not really performed its function unless, to begin with, it puts the reader in possession of the facts upon which the criticism is based, and unless--no matter upon how small a scale--its consideration is complete."

--Joseph Wood Krutch, "What Is a Good Review?" The Nation, CLXIV (April 17, 1937), 438.

WRITING ARTICLES FOR MAGAZINES AND NEWSPAPERS

Success in writing articles and getting them published, according to the writers in this section, depends on the ability of the writers to sense the interests and moods of the public, to find the right magazine for the article, to obtain the facts needed for the article, to build a suitable structure for the ideas, and to write in a pleasing manner. Such articles range in subject matter from foods to exposés, from family articles to book reviews, from personal essays to obits. Even worn-out subjects can be treated so that they are interesting to new readers. All articles must be well-written and the information must be reliable, since the people "who read significant magazines are the thinking men and women of our time."

1. Brower, Brock. "The Article," in On Creative Writing. Edited by Paul Engle. New York: E. P. Dutton and Company, Inc. Dutton Paperback, 1966, pp. 83-97.
Brower says that the impact of an article depends on the writer's individual intelligence and resolve, and not as much as formerly on the influence of the journal in which it appears. This means that the writer must do everything for himself, both the research and the interviewing. His efforts should be directed toward synthesizing the ideas of his interviewees. The writer should not set down a word on paper until he knows what he must leave unsaid. He must find a voice through which to express his ideas. For this he can learn much by listening to the voices of fiction. "What the novelists know naturally, the rest of us must learn at our pain." Brower cites George Orwell as a good example of a "voice so quietly suasive that reading him is like joining him. His articles don't end; rather, he departs, and leaves behind him both a sense of truth and a sense of embarrassment."

2. Gunther, Max. "Building a Framework for an Article," The Writer, LXXX (August, 1967), 14-16, 46.

According to Gunther, a good magazine article today must have a solid framework. "It must have a theme, make a point of some kind, drive toward a conclusion." The modern magazine article should set out to prove something. After the writer decides what he wants to prove, the next step is to determine the parts on hand to construct the proof. If they are not available, they must be found or the project must be abandoned. There is no single way to build such a structure, but Gunther illustrates his ideas by referring to the framework of one of his own articles that contained seven sections, each of which grew logically from the thesis.

3. Hochstein, Rollie. "The Personal Essay: Articles from Experience," The Writer, LXXXI (April, 1968), 9-12.

Hochstein thinks that the personal essay is a satisfactory way to get published since it requires "no research, no interviews, no scholarship, no legwork." She offers five principles that she practices in writing domestic humor pieces, the first two especially applicable to women's and family fields, the last three to all personal essays: reader identification, warm relationship with reader, disciplined thought and tight writing, a pleasing style, authoritative manner.

4. Krutch, Joseph Wood. "What Is a Good Review?" The Nation, CLXIV (April 16, 1937), 438.

Krutch says that the three minimum tasks of the book reviewer are to describe the book, to communicate something of its quality, and to pass judgment upon it. Adequate description implies a simple account of the scope and contents of the book. The communication of quality shows the impression made by the book on the mind of the reader. The description, the impression, and the judgment should be combined into an artistic whole.

5. Pringle, Henry F. "Article Writing," in The Writer's Book. Edited by Helen Hull. New York: Harper and Brothers, 1950, pp. 248-253.

The essential stock-in-trade of the writer of magazine articles is ideas. Pringle suggests that the best way to get ideas for magazine articles is to examine magazines and newspapers to learn the types of articles that have been printed, the way they were written, and their length. Weekly news magazines and technical journals may also be examined.

New and fresh approaches to old subjects are sometimes
welcome. "I am willing to gamble that there is a magazine
story in Grant's Tomb in New York, in the Kansas City,
Missouri, war memorial and in the Alamo in Texas." Travel
articles, especially those concerned with travel in the United
States, are acceptable, as well as exposés of local situations
if the writer is careful with the facts. After an idea has
been chosen, the next step is to establish contact with an
editor. The idea should be expanded into a brief outline and
sent to the editor of the magazine for which it is best suited.
If he is interested, it is good, if possible, to see him for
an interview. Pringle suggests that any one starting a free-
lance career should have some other source of income for a
year or so.

6. Rivers, William L. Free-Lancer and Staff
Writer: Writing Magazine Articles. Belmont, Calif.: Wads-
worth Publishing Company, Inc., 1972. 214 pp.
A book on magazine writing techniques of both the
free-lance and staff writer, written by an experienced writer
in these fields. The eighteen chapters are organized under
six heads: The World of the Writer, The Free-Lancer, The
Staff Writer, Free-Lancer and Staff Writer, Types of Articles,
and The Professional Writer. These chapters are followed
by three sections: "Code of Ethics and Good Practices,"
"Suggested Readings," and "Magazine Terms." Designed to
show how inexperienced and failing writers can publish consistently as free-lancers or staff writers, the book gives
concrete advice on getting ideas, landing assignments, finding
facts, and writing the article. Several of the chapters give
examples of various types of articles with detailed comments
and critiques provided in parallel columns.

7. Sissman, L. E. "Innocent Bystander: Reviewer's
Dues," Atlantic Monthly, CCXXXIV (July, 1974), 20-22. Included with some changes in The Writer, October, 1974, pp.
24-26.
Sissman found reviewing to be a difficult discipline, a
craft with its own rules and customs. He sets down a list
of twenty prohibitions that he thinks should help to guide the
reviewer in his task. They include such advice as never review the work of a friend, never read other reviews before
you write your own, never review your own ideas instead of
the author's, never fail to give the reader a judgment and
recommendation on the book, never ridicule a serious writer
on his minor errors, never write critical jargon, never fail
to take chances in judgment.

8. Weeks, Edward. "The Article," in <u>Breaking</u> <u>into Print.</u> <u>An Editor's Advice on Writing.</u> Boston: The <u>Writer, Inc.</u>, 1962, pp. 25-41.
Edward Weeks, editor of the <u>Atlantic</u> at the time, says that the ferment in the world since the 1930's has caused a demand for information that is contained in non-fiction prose, particularly in the article. Since there is much duplication in unsolicited articles sent to magazines, Weeks advises would-be writers to save themselves time and effort by sending to the editor a two-page outline of a proposed article to see if the editor is sympathetic toward the material. He also suggests that the beginner should confine his writing to local subjects that are charged with controversy, but he also says that non-controversial subjects such as food and period pieces are of interest. Good humor is almost non-existent.

9. Whitman, Alden. "So You Want to Be an Obit Writer," <u>Saturday Review,</u> LIV (December 11, 1971), 70-71.
Alden Whitman, the Chief Obituary Writer for <u>The</u> <u>New York Times,</u> explains the purpose and the method of interviewing a carefully selected number of people in advance of their death. These people are chosen according to certain criteria: the person must be sufficiently notable to rate an obituary of two columns or more; the person must be able to provide information about himself beyond what can be gathered from other sources; and he must be articulate. Whitman tells of his interviews with such people as Dean Acheson, Harry Bridges, President Ferdinand E. Marcos, Mme. Chiang Kai-shek, Theodore Reik. When interviews are conducted by mail, Whitman submits a list of questions. But he says that he always strives to transmit the man, his life, and his special flavor. To Presidents and former Presidents of the United States, the <u>Times</u> devotes four pages, or about 20,000 words; to Vice-Presidents, present and former, three pages. For everyone else, Whitman says that he tries to assess the person's importance, fame or notoriety, the public impact of his career, the interest in him as a person. Sometimes the amount of space is determined by the idea that the person is someone the readers of the <u>Times</u> should know about.

WRITING ASSIGNMENTS

1. Read Alden Whitman's "So You Want to Be an Obit Writer" and one or more of his obits in <u>The New York</u> <u>Times</u> and write a paper in which you show how he carries out

his ideas in actual articles. His obit on Dean Acheson is in the Times, Wednesday, October 13, 1971, page 50. Other accounts can be found by consulting The New York Times Index.

2. Select a book that has been recently published and write a review of it, using the ideas of Krutch and Sissman.

3. Read one of the articles in A Treasury of Great Reporting, edited by Louis L. Snyder and Richard B. Morris, 1959, and write a paper in which you analyze the article to point out its greatness.

4. Read "The Men Who Made Canoes," in Prefaces to History by Bruce Catton, 1970, pp. 169-176, and write a paper in which you describe some other creation of primitive people that shows how they were able to cope with their hostile environment. You may have to do some research before you begin.

5. Select an item of local interest and write an article about it that would be suitable for the Sunday supplement or a local newspaper or magazine. Suggested topics: a tour of places of historical interest; a visit to a street market or a broiler farm; hunting with bow and arrow; the early settlers of the community.

6. In "Discipline--Between the Cow and the Devil," Virginia Quarterly Review, L (Winter, 1974), 101-108, Louis B. Wright tells about a chore that he had as a boy, that of milking a cow to provide the family with dairy products. "I accepted my bondage to the milk stool as proof of inherited punishment for Original Sin." Write a paper in which you tell of a job or a chore that you had that provided the "iron" discipline that Wright discusses. "Nobody could weasel away from a cow." You may get some ideas from reading "Innocent Bystander, Christmas Story," by L. E. Sissman in Atlantic, CCXXXII (December, 1973), 36, 40, 42, about how he and his friend tried to sell vacuum cleaners in Northeast Vermont.

7. Read Walter Pater, "La Gioconda," in The Renaissance, Modern Library Edition, pp. 102-104, and using Pater's method of interpretation of Leonardo da Vinci's painting as a model, write your interpretation of another painting that you study while visiting an art gallery.

8. Read a book of travel and write a paper in which you discuss both the content and the form of the book. You may want to choose one of the following books, or, if you have had an interesting trip, write an account of your own travels.

John Wesley Powell:
Explorations of the Colorado River of the West, 1875.
The Romance of the Colorado River, 1902.

Frederick Law Olmstead:
A Journal in the Seaboard Slave States, 1856.
A Journey through Texas, 1857.
A Journey in the Back Country, 1863.

9. Read All the President's Men by Robert Woodward and Carl Bernstein, 1974, and write a paper in which you present what you learned from these reporters about collecting information. You should also read Max Lerner, "Writing 'Hot History,'" Saturday Review, May 29, 1976, pp. 16-19. In this article Woodward and Bernstein talk with Lerner about investigative reporting and its place in the writing of history.

10. In When in Doubt, Mumble; A Bureaucrat's Handbook (New York: Van Nostrand Company, 1972), James H. Boren, the author, satirizes the modern military-industrial-political-educational complex in the United States. Read the book and write a paper in which you pull out from the various sections of the book the basic ideas that Boren stands for as shown by his descriptions of bureaucratic behavior especially as it pertains to the use of language. You may want to discuss this book in relation to Language and Public Policy, edited by Hugh Rank. See page 166.

11. In 1938, Evelyn Waugh wrote a novel, Scoop, considered by some critics as the best satire on journalism ever written. Read the novel and write a paper on the aspects of journalism that Waugh satirizes.

AUTHOR-TITLE INDEX

198 / Author-Title Index